"It was the summer of 1956 when Don Rippy and I were engaged, looking forward to our October wedding. Don had a visiting friend named Bob Hoskins, and Hazel Crabtree was my guest. Of course conventional wisdom required an introduction... how could we possibly have known that we were instrumental in uniting a team of world changers?

...And I Sat There will take you on a trip around the entire world with this dynamic duo, following the Lord's leading with total abandonment and never seeking credit for themselves. Even though at times it's bumpy, you'll love the ride."

— **ARTHELENE RIPPY**
PRODUCER, HOST
CHRISTIAN TELEVISION NETWORK

"This remarkable woman of God has led an extraordinary life. Varied, interesting, challenging, adventuresome, and she has lived it with supernatural grace, deep faith, and a great sense of humor—which I am sure has helped get her through many a tough situation.

She and Bob started ministry together at a very young age, and they have not stopped yet. Hazel has not SAT for sure! And she has not only "stood by her man," but she has RUN along with him in this race.

What a fun read. Enjoy and be inspired by the life of one woman who said "yes" to God—a woman I am privileged to call my friend."

— **GIGI GRAHAM**
WOMEN'S SPEAKER, AUTHOR
DAUGHTER OF BILLY GRAHAM

"I couldn't help but laugh when I heard the title of my friend Hazel's new book. If there was ever an oxymoron to describe her, that is it.

I have known Hazel for many years, and keeping up with her is a real challenge. You never know where in the world you may be calling, texting or emailing her! This firecracker of a missionary, wife and mother has traveled the world devoted to spreading the message of Christ.

She is a wonderful writer, telling her stories with charm and a contagious humor. This book could only be the "tip of the iceberg" of her life experiences and—as you will discover—she didn't just SIT THERE! This book is guaranteed to be a joy to all who read it."

— **BARBARA GREEN**
CO-FOUNDER, HOBBY LOBBY

...And I Sat There

OneHope
600 SW 3rd St.
Pompano Beach, FL 33060
www.onehope.net

Cover design and text art by Hudson Phillips.

Unless otherwise noted, all Scripture quotations are from the King James Version of the Bible.

Portions of this book were previously published in *Honeymoon Safari* copyright © 1963 by Hazel Hoskins.

Grateful acknowledgment is made to Terry Raburn for permission to reprint previously published material from *Under the Guns In Beirut* copyright © 1980 by the Gospel Publishing House. Used with permission.

International Standard Book Number: 978-1-59480-966-8

Printed in the United States of America

Dedication

This book is dedicated in memory of my late parents, Clifford and Helen Crabtree. When I was a little girl, they taught me to study the Scriptures and appropriate them to the needs of my life. How I thank God for this wonderful heritage!

To my amazing husband, Bob Hoskins, to whom I quoted the words of Ruth to Naomi: "Wither thou goest, I will go." That was 54 years ago. I didn't know I would "goest" so far... and "wither" so fast. Thank you, my forever love, for an exciting life! Boring? Seldom. Unpredictable and adventuresome? Always.

. . . And to my very special children, their spouses, and their children. . .

My prayer is that you, my children and grandchildren, will experience God's wondrous love and power in your lives. If you will exercise the disciplines of reading God's Word, along with the practice of prayer and meditation, I have found that through the good times as well as the bad, His grace is sufficient.

"Trust in the Lord with all thine heart; and lean not unto thine own understanding. In all thy ways acknowledge him, and he shall direct thy paths." (Proverbs 3:5-6)

And to future generations . . .

My godly parents, Rev. Clifford and Helen Crabtree

Contents

Foreword by George Wood i

Prologue v

1. Love and Marriage 1

2. To Africa 7

3. From Nairobi to Hong Kong. 33

4. Latin America 59

5. Middle East Outreach 67

6. Vive La France!. 105

7. Life Publishers 109

8. Book of Hope 117

9. Around the World with the *Book of Hope* . . . 123

10. OneHope: Our Journey Revisited. 141

11. Return To Africa 155

Epilogue 161

Afterword by Rob Hoskins 167

Acknowledgements 171

Foreword

DR. GEORGE WOOD
SUPERINTENDENT, GENERAL COUNCIL ASSEMBLIES OF GOD

You are about to read a remarkable story written by a remarkable woman who was used of God as a hidden spring of charm and influence to play a major role behind the scenes—to give birth to and nurture one of the greatest missionary enterprises in the Christian Church in general and the Assemblies of God in particular, namely, OneHope.

Anyone who knows Hazel Hoskins would never accuse her of "sitting there" as just another spectator to a worldwide ministry that has touched more than one billion children and young people with the living and written Word of God.

Hazel received a heritage and strength from both her parents. Her father, Clifford Crabtree, became an influential Pentecostal pastor and preacher in New

England. Her mother, Helen, was known as a brilliant student and teacher of God's Word. However, spiritual life and gifting are not passed through earthly inheritance but by the Spirit Himself, which was evident in Hazel at an early age.

After Hazel's graduation from Central Bible College in Springfield, Missouri, she met and married Bob Hoskins who was called by God to preach at the age of seven, and became a well-known child evangelist. In his teen years, he began to travel the world. The Lord of the harvest used him powerfully.

The story of the Hoskins, as a married couple, begins in Africa and is recounted by Hazel in her book *Honeymoon Safari*. From there the reader is taken in this book on a breathtaking life-journey of missionary evangelism around the world; a ten year assignment living in Beirut, Lebanon; and five years living in France, with a continued outreach to the Middle East.

The book *...And I Sat There* culminates with the inside story of OneHope that God is using today to influence the leaders of nations, religion and commerce to reach the children of the world. When you have finished reading this book, you will have to say "He is building His Church" in spite of human barriers, false religions and Satanic strategies.

Prologue

We were in Colorado for a missions convention and Bob, as usual, preached his heart out during a Sunday morning service. Afterwards, a lady came up to me and said,

"Your husband, he's so wonderful."

I agreed, "Yes, it's true."

"How does he do all he does?"

"I don't know. I get tired just following him around."

To which she replied:

"AND YOU JUST SIT THERE..."

"Well," I thought. "It's nice to be recognized for what I do best, and if I ever write a book, that will be the title."

Many wives married to high-profile men find themselves in similar situations. When you attend a church for the first time, the man of God (your husband) is ushered to the inner sanctum (the pastor's office). You? Well, you're left to find your own way.

My friend Millie Triplett, whose husband Loren was the Foreign Missions Director of the Assemblies of God, once found herself in this situation. She struck up a conversation with a friendly soul and thought to herself, "Guess I'll sit with her." Millie ended up in the choir loft!

It's all a bit facetious, but when we stand before God at the judgment, He will ask each one of us, "What did you do with the talents I gave YOU?"

"My husband did exploits in your Name, and well, I sat there..." is not an acceptable response—at least not for me!

We are each responsible to utilize whatever gifts we have to fulfill the Great Commission, whether on a platform of popularity or in an obscure place where no one knows our name or sees our deeds.

This book is a compilation of observations and impressions gathered through the years; some in the form of articles; others expressed in poetry.

In Charles Krauthammer's book, *Things That Matter*, he wrote, "When I married my wife, Robyn, she co-authored my life." Obviously, if I hadn't married Bob Hoskins on September 5, 1959, this book would have turned out in the book of Habakkuk one morning, chapter two, verse three jumped out at me:

> *"For the VISION is yet for an appointed time, but at the end, it shall speak, and not lie; though it tarry, wait for it; because it will surely come, it will not tarry."*
> *(Habakkuk 2:3)*

(After I met Bob and related this Scripture to him, he responded with expansive gesticulations, "and I am THE VISION.")

The same day I was reading the Scripture in Habakkuk, my mother was reading the book of Ruth and felt that Naomi's admonition to Ruth was just for me:

> *"Sit still, my daughter, until thou know how the matter will fall; for the man, (Boaz) will not be in rest, until he has finished the thing this day."*
> *(Ruth 3:18)*

These two Scriptures encouraged me to "just sit there" and wait, because the VISION was forthcoming.

I decided the only sitting I was going to do would be on a traveling piano bench. I accepted an invitation from

CHAPTER 1

Love and Marriage

In 1954, I graduated from Central Bible College with a degree in Bible and an engagement to be married to a fine young man shortly thereafter. At my home in Maine, while preparing for the June wedding, I modeled my wedding dress for my parents. Descending the winding staircase in all my finery, my dad took one look at my face, and said, "You're the saddest looking bride-to-be I've ever seen!" Bursting into tears, I responded, "You're right, dad, I highly respect my fiancé, but don't love him enough to spend the rest of my life with him." My very wise father advised, "Then break it off right now." Which I did. . .

The ensuing months at home, with no possible suitor on the horizon, were filled with despondency. Surely I was destined to be an "old maid" or one of "God's unclaimed jewels."

With nothing but time on my hands, I enrolled at the New England Conservatory of Music in Bangor, Maine to pursue my degree in piano performance. I also spent much time in prayer for guidance as to my future. Reading

Our first adventure of married
life—cutting the cake!

quite differently. This visionary, entrepreneur and—most importantly—man of God is my co-author.

the public relations director for Central Bible College to arrange, and travel as the accompanist, for a musical group representing the school.

Upon the conclusion of that tour in 1955, Arthelene Rippy, (nee' McClure), asked me to accompany her to Arkansas to visit her fiancé, Don Rippy. Don's friend, Bob Hoskins, was also in Arkansas filling in for a vacationing pastor. "Lene" deployed me to occupy Don's friend, Bob, so they could focus on their wedding plans. Enter: THE VISION.

The week after we met, it just "so happened" that we were both attending a conference in Oklahoma City. Bob invited me out for dinner, which led to some months of correspondence. In one of his letters, he informed me that he would be in the Northeast and would love to preach for my dad. Having never heard Bob preach, I didn't know what I was getting dad's parishioners into. But I took a step of faith, and was not disappointed. In fact, I was very proud, as this smart young preacher boy was very eloquent!

Our courtship consisted of ongoing letters via "snail mail." Bob left the United States for a year of evangelism in South and East Africa, while I accepted a position on staff at Bethel Temple in Sacramento, California as scriptwriter for the TV show, "Our Story," and as pianist.

During our time apart, I incorporated the lyrics to a then-popular song into one of my letters to Bob:

"See the pyramids along the Nile.
Watch the sunrise on a tropic isle;
Just remember, darling, all the while,
YOU BELONG TO ME"
- Patsy Cline

In his time ministering in Africa, Bob contracted malaria. After suffering a raging fever alone in a hotel room for three days, he came to the realization that, in such situations, he might benefit from having some wifely companionship. His return to the United States brought with it a proposal where he asked me to be his wife. That's where it all began...

Although my husband had been ministering to large audiences since the age of seven, and had conducted a marriage ceremony at age ten, his own wedding proved to be a different proposition! When it came time for us to recite our memorized marriage vows, his mind went blank. I nervously mouthed the phrases to prompt him. Of course he emphatically denies this and claims that he was simply pausing for dramatic effect! Either way, it was official—we were married in Sacramento, California on September 5, 1959.

1959 Bethel Temple, Sacramento, CA.
Our wedding party (from left)

Bridesmaids: Charlotte Ann Crabtree; Joan; Jolene Hoskins; Arthelene McClure; Irene Baily; Ramona Crabtree; Jacque Johnson

Groomsmen: Charles Crabtree; Bill Johnson; Loren Cunningham; Don Rippy; Elmer Bueno; Mark Davidson; John York

Playing the accordion at an open
air crusade in Tamale, Ghana

CHAPTER 2

To Africa

1960

Six months later, on March 11, 1960, we woke to a cold yet invigorating day in the city of Boston. The residents were recovering from the worst snowstorm in ninety years. Icicles glittered in the morning sun, then plummeted down to the slushy streets. Gigantic mounds of snow began to melt, morphing into the shapes of vehicles that had been buried below. People happily slushed to work in anticipation of soon being able to shed their fur-lined boots.

I awoke with feelings alternating between exhilaration and apprehension. We had been looking forward to this day for so long, and now it was finally here! We were done with the days of endless paper shuffling, visits to offices to apply for passports and visas and to purchase airplane tickets. My aching arm reminded me that I had received all of the necessary inoculations and vaccinations every overseas traveler must endure. I had crammed as much drip-dry, wrinkle resistant, wash and wear clothing as I could into our forty-four pound luggage allowance. The "dainty" items, such as film, face cream and reading material were tightly packed into my handbag. Despite careful planning, we had slightly exceeded the luggage allowance, but it didn't matter. We were ready to GO!

Little did we know when we planned this trip, that we would be going not only to West and East Africa, but would be starting a journey that would end up taking us around the world.

We have always trusted that God would go ahead of us and prepare the way. But to actually walk down the path, then turn and look back to see the dangers He kept us safe from is a faith-deepening experience.

When we arrived at the airport, we were slightly perturbed that the travel agent had not yet delivered our tickets, especially when our departure time was drawing near. We later found out that if we had left at the time we had originally planned, we would have been in Agadir, Morocco, during the devastating earthquake that killed 3,000 people. God was watching over us, indeed!

Settled on the plane at last, our huge steel bird rose into the clouds that bore close resemblance to the great mounds of snow we had just left behind. Below us, the sea's rippling gave off the effect of an interminable cobblestone street. Behind us, was the jagged outline of Boston containing our family, friends and all things familiar. Ahead of us was an expanse of ocean leading to the unknown…

FIRST NIGHT IN AFRICA
SENEGAL

Missionary Talmadge Butler flew us in his Beechcraft Bonanza airplane high over the flat, arid terrain of Senegal in French West Africa. We could see hundreds of little villages scattered intermittently below—villages where the name of Jesus had yet to be heard. Our destination was the township of Keduga, more than three hundred miles in the interior.

As our plane bounced over the rough ground that formed the makeshift "runway," many of the younger inhabitants of the village ran to greet us. We left the plane on the outskirts of Keduga and an intoxicated Frenchman drove us into town in his truck. After a rather insipid Bunsen burner meal, washed down with warm lemonade, we piled into a Willys Jeep. We bounced over sticks and rocks until we arrived at an adjoining village.

The women of the village were busy washing at the river.

First they would wash the clothes they had on and lay them on rocks to dry. Then, they would wash the things they had brought with them, and lastly they would wash their grain. However, on that day, when they heard us play a phonograph record in their local dialect, they left their clothes to soak in the river and came running. It didn't take long for the entire population to gather in the largest grass hut.

After playing the record, we told the story of Jesus and His love to the nearly nude natives surrounding us. A young lad had agreed to interpret for us, but he refused to repeat the Name of Jesus…Islam had already found its way to this remote village, and he was afraid to say the Name of Jesus for fear of persecution. We decided to pray for the sick in the village asking God to reveal His power through healings. We left confident that God would vindicate His Name in that village, and that many would come to know the reality of Christ.

After being in 112-degree temperatures all day, we looked forward to a refreshing bath and good night's sleep at the government rest house. However, when I saw the unsanitary (to put it mildly) conditions, I almost stayed in the Jeep! Filth and fatigue won out, and I very timorously showered before crawling under the dusty mosquito net for some much-needed rest.

It was hot and dry and there was a full moon that night. As we lay on the dirty sheet, we could hear the deep throbbing of drums. Bob whispered to me, "the natives are restless because there are visitors in their village." He was teasing me, of course. When there is a full moon, Africans dance all night to keep the evil spirits away.

Far into the night, we watched the tribe gyrate in the moonlight, listening to the monotonous beating of the drums, indicative of the emptiness and hollowness of the human heart without Christ.

I WILL BUILD MY CHURCH
SIERRA LEONE

Our next stop was 350 miles into the interior of Sierra Leone, the village of Koindu. The pounding rain beat a fast staccato on the tin roof of the church on the hill; the flickering lights of the kerosene lanterns cast shadows on the group of believers kneeling at the humble altar of roughly-hewn logs.

We had planned an open-air service at the center of activity—the marketplace—but thought the tropical storm that came at service time rather inconvenient to outdoor evangelism. Through the blinding rains, the people trekked to the church with their benches on their heads, the lightning flashes illuminating their way.

It was Sunday night. As I sat toward the back of this unpretentious place of worship, I thought of the thousands of Christians all over the world who at that moment were kneeling at an altar of prayer: our loved ones in America; believers in China, India, the Islands of the Sea; and these precious Africans, their dark faces glowing with light from an inward source. This verse that kept coming to my mind, "I WILL BUILD MY CHURCH, and the gates of Hell shall not prevail against it..." (Matthew 16:18)

Just three years prior, these people had been persecuted like the early Christians. Because they had burned their fetishes, the enraged members of the secret society beat them unmercifully, cut gashes in their heads, and poured hot coals in the open wounds. Numbers of them were imprisoned for many months. As I looked at Moses, the pastor, who had received the greatest amount of persecution, I thought of what he had told us the day before. He said he had felt no pain, but thought only of the price Jesus had paid for the forgiveness of his sins.

Our services in Koindu would long be remembered.

The trials and afflictions of the Kissi people had made them strong and fearless. Many received the Holy Spirit and, with great zeal, went into the towns and villages to witness. They frequently returned to preach in the village where they received their beatings.

THE PALM WINE TRANSLATOR

The following week after that stormy Sunday, we went with Pastor Moses to another village to plant a church. It seemed there was no one in the village that could translate from English into the local dialect. When we were about to give up, an inebriated man, dirty and shabbily dressed, said that he could translate for us.

Bob preached in English and the gentleman translated into the local dialect. He translated like "a house afire." After the service, Bob told him, "You did great. Come back tomorrow night; clean up a bit, and lay off the palm wine."

He did so, appearing in a black suit and tie with a white starched shirt…sober as a judge! However, to quote my mother, "He couldn't preach a hen off a nest." We felt like telling him to take a little nip. Yet, we left confident that God honors His Word in spite of the messenger.

OUR FIRST HOME
LIBERIA

Since Liberia has very few roads, airplanes are the exclusive method for interior travel. Early missionaries were carried by bearer-drawn hammocks, a method which took many days and was extremely exhausting. We were much too new-fangled for the hammocks, so we flew to reach our destination of Feloka in Liberia. It seemed as if we were dropping straight out of the sky and might scrape the tops of the tall mahogany trees seconds before bouncing onto the airstrip that doubled as the "main street" of Feloka. At the end of the airstrip sat our first home.

I wonder how many newlywed brides would envy me my first home? Who wouldn't dream of living in a mud house with a thatched roof? Or envision being carried across a threshold that was washed with cow dung every morning? What about cooking on a wood stove by the light of a kerosene lamp every single night?

The cooking went fine, but I had a little trouble the first time I tried "milking the cow." Our only option for dairy was mixing powdered milk flakes with water, and by the dim light of the kerosene lamp, I must have mistaken the flour tin for the powdered milk tin. The color of the "milk" was right, but the pasty texture left much to be desired...There may or may not have been another disaster the first time I tried to give my dear husband a haircut, but let's forego the details on that one…

Milk and haircut mishaps aside, we thanked God for a spirit of revival in the morning chapel services at the elementary school, and also in the evening meetings in Feloka town. One native woman with a baby strapped on her back gave her child quite a ride during her baptism. All we could see was the baby's fuzzy little head bobbing up and down in the water!

HOW BEAUTIFUL THE FEET

It was June in Liberia, which means almost continual downpour. But the rain didn't stop "Papa" Fred. I saw him coming down the muddy road—a tall, commanding figure wearing a khaki cap and coat. I was enamored with his feet.

The only protection his feet had against the rocky, wet terrain were the heavy callouses that were beginning to form yellow "soles." His fascinating feet were off on a trek that would take Papa Fred to many of the villages under his jurisdiction as superintendent of the Assemblies of God churches in Liberia. Those same feet would also take him to preach the Gospel of peace to many who had never heard.

This old man—a title of high respect in Liberia—had told me his story:

> *"My father was the high priest of a devil society. Since my ambition was to be like my father, I was always present when he made sa acrifice. I watched every movement. Probably the most enticing feature to me was that the high priest always got the best meat of the sacrifice. After he had partaken of his juicy morsel, the poorer grades of meat would be doled out to the other villagers, at which time "the devil" would hide in the bush and throw stones at the hapless villagers. They would scream, "Devil! Devil!" and run for their huts, leaving their meat for "the devil" and his family.*
>
> *Missionaries came to Newaka, our village, in 1906. My father hated them because they were taking away much of his business, so I did too. We did everything we could to make life as uncomfortable as possible for them. When many of them died of black water fever, we were very happy.*
>
> *One day in August of 1916, I took my cutlass and climbed a palm tree in search of nuts. After perching myself on a high limb, I prepared to indulge in one of my many evils: dipping snuff. First, I dropped a portion out of the tree for "the devil," and was ready for a dip myself when I had a*

vision. I was standing on a great mountain and below me was a horrible pit in which many people were screaming and crying. Right then I realized if I didn't give my heart to God, I would end up in that awful place. I was so frightened that I left the palm nuts and the snuff in the tree for "the devil," and ran to the mission station. I gave my heart and life to God, and the following week was gloriously filled with the Spirit. This was the most wonderful experience of my life.

My father was so angry when he found out what had happened to me he said he never wanted to see my face again. If he died he didn't want me to come to his funeral, and if I died, he would be glad.

The persecution I encountered during the next few years was even worse than what my father and I had inflicted upon the missionaries. Our lives were threatened many times by secret societies because so many of their members turned to Christ, burning their ju-ju's and fetishes.

I have lived to see my son, Samuel, follow in my footsteps, teaching in the Bible school, and preaching the Gospel in the surrounding towns and villages."

Through the rain, I watched the solitary figure until he was out of sight. "Papa Fred, you will never be a fetish high priest, but you ARE a priest. A priest unto God," I thought.

"How beautiful are the feet of them that preach the gospel of peace, and bring glad tidings of good things!" (Romans 10:15).

LETTER FROM A "DEJOBBED" PERSON

This letter was given to me in Freetown, Sierra Leone, by Mrs. John Kennedy, who served with her husband as a missionary there. It is the passionate appeal for "rejobulation" of a dismissed employee to his former employer. I am sure the author of this letter did not mean for us to giggle at its contents, but we did. And can you imagine if a letter like this were to be circulated today? (Note: misspellings intentionally retained to preserve the spirit of the letter)

Kind Sir,

On the opening of this letter, you will behold the work of a dejobbed person, and a very bewifed and much-childrenized gentleman who was violently dejobbed in a twinkling by your good self.

For heaven's sake, sir, consider this catastrophy as falling on your own head, and remind yourself as walking home at the month's end to five savage wives and sixteen ferocious children with a pocketful of non-existent shillings, and sixpence. Not one solitary penny, pity my horrible state!

When being dejobbed and proceeding with a heart and intestines filled with misery to this den of home, myself did greedily contemplate culpable homicide, but Him who protected Daniel in the lion's den will protect this servant in this home of evil.

As to the reason given by yourself, Esquire, for my debjobbment, the incriminations was laziness...No Sir! It was impossible that myself who has pitched sixteen infant children into this valley of tears can have a lazy atom in his mortal frame, and the departure of 11 monthly shillings have left me on the verge of the abyss of destitution and despair.

I hope this vision of horror will enrich your dreams this night and good angels will meet and pulverize your heart of nether millstone so that you will awaken, and with much alacrity as might be compatible with your personal safety, and hasten to rejobulate your servant.

So mite it be, Amen.
Yours despairfully,
Anonymous

SIGNS AND WONDERS AT THE TAMALE CRUSADES GHANA

Thousands of Africans representing many tribes, wealthy Lebanese merchants, and missionaries of various denominations were all gathered in the lorry park. We were about to hold the first evangelistic crusade that had ever been conducted in this strong Muslim center. Little did we know the signs and wonders we would see during this crusade.

National workers and missionaries reported talking and praying with at least fifty adults each night in the "prayer and conversion" tent. Mass children's altar calls were also being conducted in an adjoining prayer tent. We thought we had taught the children to sing the crusade chorus, "I'm so glad Jesus lifted me," but soon realized the crowd was getting a good laugh at the little ones' performance as they actually sang, "I'm so BAD Jesus lifted me."

A man named Whitlow had come to the crusade hoping to find relief for his hand, which had a severe tropical infection and was nothing more than a swollen mass. He sobbed in pain as we began to pray for his healing. When we opened our eyes after "Amen," the swelling had

The response among the people to our crusades in Ghana was incredible!

completely disappeared and the infection had dried up. What a wonder!

One lad who accepted Christ at the meetings told us that his Muslim dad beat him each night after he returned home from the lorry park. This beaten boy faithfully attended each night and brought his unsaved friends with him. God granted him strong faith right from the beginning!

During one of the concluding services in Tamale, four prostitutes of the Dagomba tribe accepted Christ into their lives. The morning after their conversion, they came to us at the missions compound to request prayer that

God would give them new jobs and new homes. While in prayer, the presence of the Lord filled the room and three of the women received glorious baptisms in the Spirit.

One of the women became so overjoyed during her Spirit baptism that she danced about the room and said in perfect English with no accent whatsoever, "My mother didn't teach me, my father didn't teach me, but Jesus you taught me about you!" After she finished her dance and sat down, we asked her if she could speak English. She had to turn to the woman next to her, who spoke limited English, and ask what we had said!

On another occasion in the primitive Bassari, Toto, area, an illiterate bush woman quoted the 23rd Psalm, verbatim, in flawless English while receiving the baptism of the Spirit.

The oldest woman of the group described a vision she had received. Through the interpreter she said, "I saw two roads, one—a rocky, stony road with a great fire at the end of it; the other—a narrow, clean way. A short man tried to get me on the rocky road, but all of a sudden, a big white bird swooped down upon me, carried me off and put me on the clean road. The bird flew over me and I felt safe."

It was wonderful to witness God revealing himself to those who had been in total spiritual darkness. One night during the service, an African man kept trying to gain Bob's attention. When my husband finally recognized him, the man said, "I have a house that is not being used. God has been speaking to me all day to offer two rooms in my house to someone who is in need." God had not only provided for the spiritual needs of these people, but for their material needs as well.

When the meetings from the lorry park came to an end, the attendees transitioned from the park site to the church building via a large parade, which wound its way through the city streets. During the last week of the crusade, the new converts were taught about the Holy Spirit. I overheard one of the African Christian men remark that, "The whole condition of Tamale has been changed by these open air meetings."

The Africans often gave names to people representative of how they perceived them. Bob was dubbed "the man of faith," and it stuck.

THE FERTILITY PRAYER
NIGERIA

In Africa, if you've been married nine months and one day, a child should be on the way momentarily.

We were ministering in a little village church in Jos, Nigeria. Bob had finished preaching and I was "just sitting there"—as I was wont to do—on a rough-hewn log.

The pastor concluded the service with prayer and after fervently praying for Bob, his prayers turned my direction. In his thick accent, he passionately (and loudly) pleaded,

> *"Dear Lawd, bless the missus. Lawd God of Han-nah;*
> *Lawd God of Sa-rah, Open dis heah woman's womb*
> *TONIGHT, Lawd."*

The next morning, the pastor carried the little cloth bag containing the previous night's offering up to the mission compound to be counted. After visiting with Bob and the missionary, he inquired, "And how's the missus?"

Bob told him, "She's not feeling too well this morning."

To which he shouted, *Bwana Yesu Asafiwe* ("PRAISE DE LAWD!" in Swahili).

He thought the Lord had answered his prayer right away… but truth be told it was nothing more than a mild case of dysentery. It wasn't until three years later that our first son, David, would be born.

TO EAST AFRICA
TANZANIA

We left Accra, Ghana, July 4th, 1961, after more than a year in West Africa. In Nairobi, Kenya, we boarded a rickety bus bound for Arusha, Tanganyika, (now Tanzania). The Tanganyika District Council of the Assemblies of God would be held at Arusha, and we were looking forward to enjoying five delightful days of fellowship and inspiration with missionaries and national workers.

The "road trip" from Nairobi to Arusha afforded us the opportunity to see much of what American journalist, John Gunther, referred to in his book *Inside Africa* as "the wonderful world of Tanganyika." As we bounced along, we took in great rolling country, overarched by a brilliantly blue sky. Several times, our vehicle swerved violently in order to avoid hitting a zebra or the more protracted giraffe.

As we neared Arusha, Mount Meru came into view with its shafts of fleecy, white clouds piercing the top. In the distance, we espied the snowy summit of Kilimanjaro rising from the plains to its majestic height of nearly 20,000 feet. We found the higher altitude very invigorating after the enervating humidity of West Africa.

Despite his heavy preaching schedule, Bob found time

Bob the hunter with his warthog trophy!

to go hunting with missionary friend Paul Bruton and was able to attain some beautiful trophies. While visiting the Old Boma taxidermy museum in Arusha, Bob met Ernest Hemingway's son, Patrick, and also John Wayne who was there for the filming of *Hatari*. (Perhaps you remember Henry Mancini's musical theme for the movie, "Baby Elephant Walk"?)

Meanwhile, instead of "just sitting there" at the Bruton home, I taught teenaged Sally Bruton how to drive. Let's just say the hunters weren't the only ones to eliminate some of God's beautiful creatures that day.

After the council, we held a series of meetings with Paul and Helen Bruton, which resulted in a church plant. The Brutons had built a beautiful "contemporary" (for 1961) church with a glass wall. I remember sitting on the front pew looking out the glass wall when I saw a Masai warrior, spear in hand, approach with intent to enter the building.

His face was daubed with red ocher paint, his hair "set" with cow dung and his pierced ear lobes had been stretched with large metal rings. The gourd on his back contained blood drawn from the neck of a living cow through a reed mixed with curdled milk, the diet of the Masai.

As this tall, lean Masai tried to enter the church, the glass wall obstructed him. He drew back and began to attack the invisible barrier! After several tries, he finally figured his "enemy" out, and realized that to enter the church, he would need to do so through the door. I still chuckle at this rather humorous example of extreme cultural difference.

Paul Bruton shared an old Masai warrior's words to him: "Bwana, when one has been in the darkness so long, it takes a long time to get used to the light. Please tell us again, slowly, slowly . . ."

I watched the young man sitting beside me try to grasp the simple Gospel story told by "Bwana" Hoskins, as he heard for the first time about the Son of God, who could take away his sins.

Interesting note: Ghana received independence from Great Britain during the time we were there, and Kwame Nkrumah became its first president. Nigeria received its independence in 1960. Jomo Kenyatta, considered the brains of the Mau-Mau, was released from prison during our stay in Kenya. Although I don't think we had anything to do with the political independence, I know for certain that we played a part in the spiritual deliverance that took place there.

GOD MAKES A PATH
KENYA

Nairobi is the capital of Kenya, a modern metropolis with scurrying shoppers and traffic jams. Its population is comprised of Africans, Asians, and Europeans. The colony achieved notoriety in 1952 as the scene of the brutal Mau Mau uprisings. "Within a Lion's Roar" was the motto on the New Stanley Hotel located in the heart of the city, less than five miles from Kenya's most popular game reserve.

Canadian missionaries to Nairobi, Paul and Mary
Ann Hawkes. Ready for the evening crusade!

Through our PAOC (Pentecostal Assemblies of Canada) contact in Kenya—missionaries Paul and Mary Anne (nee' Plymire) Hawkes—we were able to secure a strategic site for our revival tent. We set up at the traffic circle where Nairobi's two busiest boulevards converged.

During the next two weeks, several hundred people responded to the invitation to receive Jesus. These included tall, white-bearded Indians in turbans, prominent English settlers, and African schoolteachers. People sent letters and telegrams to relatives and friends throughout the colony, and some came from as far away as Uganda. Roy Rogers and Dale Evans, in Kenya on safari, were guests at one of the evening services.

While in Nairobi, there were accounts in the newspapers of the homes of settlers being broken into, usually by members of the Kikuyu tribe, while inhabitants were attending the tent revivals. We were startled to see the picture of 18-year old Vicki Mann, a member of the most famous game trapping family, on the front page of the newspaper one morning. The Manns had been very faithful in attending the tent revival. The account said that eight Africans, armed with machetes and pangas, broke into the Mann home while Vicki was home alone. As they tried to force her into the bedroom, she saw an opening and dashed for a nearby closet, which had an inside lock. Terrorized, she stayed there until her family returned from the tent crusade to find the house ransacked and many valuables stolen. Vicki gave God all the credit for her protection. The headline caption read, "God Made a Path." This tribe of one million eventually became infected with the Mau Mau plague.

The usual schedule for our crusades was to spend the last week in the local church. This time, we were in a newly completed revival center where new converts could receive training and discipleship under the local leadership. It was thrilling to see people of many different nationalities worshiping side by side in a land shredded and torn by racial strife.

We have returned several times to East Africa. To see the results of planted seed is so rewarding.

September, 1960—Bob and I in Ghana,
celebrating our first wedding anniversary

CHAPTER 3
From Nairobi to Hong Kong

❦

1961

We said goodbye to the vast continent of Africa in October of 1961, nearly twenty months after our arrival.

We returned to America six months later by a rather circuitous route. Our journey took us east to Ceylon, India, Burma, Malaysia, Bali, and Hong Kong. We ministered along the way, sowing seed for the establishment of churches, many of which are still flourishing today.

THE PEARL OF THE INDIAN OCEAN CEYLON

The moment we stepped onto the Boeing 707 Jetliner, which conveyed us to populous Bombay, we began to absorb much of the flavor of the East. Lovely dark-skinned stewardesses in colorful saris served us the inevitable chicken curry, the heat of which neither our palates, nor our stomachs, ever became quite accustomed to. After a short stopover in Bombay, we departed for our first meeting in Southeast Asia on the sultry island of Ceylon.

After the ordeal of clearing through customs, during which I thought they were going to count the buttons on my husband's shirt, we boarded a bus transporting us thirty miles into the heart of Colombo, the capital. Although night was falling, we could see much of the scenery that has made Ceylon the "Pearl of the Indian Ocean." A land of waving palms, picturesque fishing boats and tropical fruits, the island ranks as the second largest producer of tea. Religiously, about two-thirds of the Ceylonese are Buddhists. Yellow-robed priests and Buddhist temples dot every landscape.

Although people of all ages attended, the meetings were characterized by a special movement of the Spirit among the young people. Laden with handbills advertising the meetings, the youngsters went from house to house and preached on street corners. Their efforts were rewarded! Despite heavy rains, the building was packed every night—ushers reported that hundreds were unable to gain entrance. Among those in attendance were relatives of the then-Prime Minister, Srima Bandaranaike—the first-ever female head of government.

Many new consecrations were made as young people poured out their hearts in fervent prayer, completely surrendering their lives to God. One young man was turned out of his home after his conversion. His family told him that if he persisted in attending "that church," he was not to come back home. His determination to hold fast to his newfound faith was revealed in his desire to be baptized at the first opportunity.

Missionary Cecil Good, sponsor of the revival, stated, "In over thirty years as an Assemblies of God minister, this was the most inspirational youth emphasis I have ever witnessed."

EVER LEARNING...NEVER COMING TO A KNOWLEDGE
INDIA

Cinders from the coal-burning engine flew into our eyes. The air was stifling, and the seats were hard. Finally, the train slammed to a halt and we piled out for lunch. Vendors with trays of samosas (the Indian version of a Mexican taco), papadums (similar to tortillas, but made with wheat instead of corn), sweet tea with milk, and bananas displayed their wares to the hungry flies and contaminated air. Although dubious about the cleanliness of the food, we were so ravenous that we contributed a few

Bob and I departing for India

rupees and returned to our compartment to consume a meal we found fairly edible.

We were en route from Madras to Bangalore, sharing our small compartment with three Hindus. They had all received their educations in the United States and were apparently highly successful in their chosen professions. When they discovered the nature of our visit to India, the subject of discussion immediately turned to that of religion.

The greatest enigma to them regarding Christianity

was the element of faith. Hinduism is a religion of works. Perfection is attained through study, concentration, and physical suffering. I asked one of the men, the youngest of the group, how one would know if they reached Utopia. He cited the case of a yogi man who, by looking at you, knew how you were constituted and, if you needed healing, he could perform a miracle through his tremendous powers of concentration. This man, through constant effort and through keeping his mind and body under complete subjection, had finally attained to what was the ultimate in spiritual experience as far as the young Hindu was concerned. These "successful" men appeared to me to epitomize those whom Paul described as "ever learning, but never able to come to a knowledge of the truth" in 2 Timothy 3:7.

As we neared Bangalore, we left the green, marshy rice land and came into cooler, more mountainous country. During the three weeks we spent in Bangalore, we ministered at the Southeast Asia Bible Institute. Students came from all over India, as well as Ceylon, Fiji, Malaya and other countries of Southeast Asia to attend. We conducted evangelistic meetings in the local church during the evening, where workers personally ministered to more than 200 new converts during the campaign.

India is a land of tremendous contrast. In the midst of its pathetic poverty live some of the world's richest men. Rising above its humble hovels are some of the world's most beautiful buildings, the most famed of which is located in Agra. The Taj Mahal, a magnificent idyll in white marble inset with rubies, emeralds, garnets and jasper, was built by Shah Jahan as an immortal tribute to undying love in memory of his beloved wife, Mumtaz Mahal. Beggars sit at the gate of this excessive shrine begging for money.

We were in Bangalore during Divali, the Festival of Lights. The Hindus believe that on this night the souls of the good dead return to visit their earthly haunts. Houses are cleaned and all is made ready, as if for guests. Old earthen lamps are thrown away and replaced with new ones. The new lamps are burned all night while the entire family stays up to receive the spirits of their deceased, not yet reborn.

As we drove up and down the streets to the accompaniment of firecrackers, and viewed myriad lights shining from window ledges and terraces, our hearts were sad to think of the 450 million Indians generating light, but still trapped in darkness.

A frail little man, Mahatma Ghandi, called for political independence and received it by declaring a fast unto death. While India may be politically free, it is still in slavery to Satan and Hindu's 330 million gods. How we need to pray for light for India's night.

ON THE ROAD TO MANDALAY MYANMAR

Rangoon, "the Garden City of the East," is the sultry former capital of Burma, presently Myanmar.

Dominating the center of the city is the Shwedagon Pagoda, a towering spire of shimmering gold, its crown embedded with 5,000 diamonds. The pagoda is a glittering symbol to the millions of Buddhists in Burma.

Burma became quite famous during the Second World War as an entrance to China. The Japanese were sinking most of the supply boats headed for China, so the defenders had to come through the back door. "The Road to Mandalay," immortalized by Rudyard Kipling, was extended across Burma and into China. It became commonly known as the Burma Road. Thousands of military trucks carried supplies over the route that required sixteen months for a labor force of 200,000 Chinese and

Burmese laborers to build.

Located on the "Road to Mandalay" is the University of Burma. The beautiful, modernistic University Dome was the site of our "spiritual invasion."

Wealthy businessmen, professional people and university students were among the thousands in attendance at the meetings. Saffron-robed monks with shaved heads sat in yoga-like positions on the front row each night. People came on foot, in cars, busses, on bicycles and in "jeepies." These glorified jeeps are relics from the war. Bedecked with crepe paper and painted in vivid colors, they provided a cheap means of transportation for thousands of Burmese.

On the concluding night, 127 individuals came forward for salvation. Among the testimonies of healing was that of an old man crippled by a stroke. He was delivered instantly during the healing prayer.

At the invitation of the head monk, we proclaimed Christ as the world's only Savior at the city's largest monastery. Upon entering the monastery, we were asked to remove our shoes. This is the usual procedure when visiting shrines or "holy places" in the East. However, I noticed the monks kept their shoes on, since they are considered "holy men."

The monks had enjoyed the music in the church services they attended, and requested that I bring the accordion and play for them. I have never played under more unique conditions. Not only did the "squeeze box" accordion seem an undignified instrument to be playing in a monastery, it was equally as unusual for me to be playing in my stocking feet! Trying to garner inspiration from their faces, I noticed that they kept their eyes glued to the floor. However, after each number, they resounded with loud applause. I couldn't get by with less than five selections!

I found out later through our interpreter—a converted monk—that monks are not allowed to look at or have any physical contact with a woman. This explained their surprised expressions when I shook hands with each of them!

For two and one-half hours, my husband preached to them on the subject, "Who Is This?" proclaiming Jesus as "the Christ of the Eternities," "The Christ of the Virgin Birth," "the Christ of Miracles," "the Christ of the Resurrection and Ascension," and "the Christ of the Second Coming." They listened in rapt attention and after the service asked many questions. Of particular interest to them was the message of the Second Coming. Many stated that they felt a Redeemer would come, but they didn't know who it would be.

After the service, the head monk treated us to bread and tea. As monks are not to eat after 12 o'clock noon, he instead chewed betel. The chewing of the betel nut is the first gesture of hospitality, and the main social pastime in many parts of Asia. To chew betel, a piece of the green nut of the betel palm is dabbed with a little lime, wrapped in pepper leaves and the whole packet chewed together with a large wad of shredded tobacco that is held under a protruding lower lip. The combination of betel and lime produces an abundant flow of saliva, red as blood, and the betel addict spits constantly, leaving crimson splotches wherever he goes. Today, betel chewing is not favored by the younger generation, not only because it looks so disagreeable, but because it spoils the teeth. The older the person, the fonder he is of betel, and the ingredients are always kept on hand in boxes with little compartments, or in special satchels of woven pandanus. The betel and lime are presented to guests in little ready-made packages decorated with streamers of cut-out palm leaf.

Before we made our departure, the monks were very insistent that we visit the adjoining monastery and meet one of the oldest, most respected monks. This time, we were asked to remove our shoes in the courtyard. The "sacred" cow made his contribution to my already soiled hosiery.

The obese, eighty-three-year old abbot was seated on a gold-covered throne and flanked by several "ladies-in-waiting," who the monks explained were his "sisters." However, they bore no family resemblance.

After my husband shook hands with this dignitary, the head monk urged me forward to follow suit. As I approached the recluse, he shrank back in feigned horror, while the monks doubled over with howls of laughter.

As compensation for lack of reciprocation to my friendly gesture, we were presented with a box of stale English "biscuits" and an orange apiece, so all was not lost.

Burma, as usual, was hot and humid the day we left. Among those to see us off at the airport was one of our interpreters, Mr. Sompothin, and his grandson. The child had been given to his grandfather by his parents who thought the boy ill-fated because he was born on the thirteenth day of the month, the same day as Lord Buddha. He waved his little brown hand vigorously as our plane took off for Thailand.

Note: after several years of cruel dictatorship, the doors of Burma (now Myanmar) have opened.

THAIPUSAM
MALAYSIA

The temperature was 107 degrees. The sweating, gyrating figure in the street was being jerked and pulled by ropes that were tied to hooks gouged in his flesh. In his body were more than one hundred spears, supporting a kavadi or altar. With each step, the spears penetrated still deeper into his skin. A pin had been pushed through his swollen, protruding tongue.

We were witnessing the horrible Hindu festival Thaipusam in Ipoh, Malaya. Considered one of the most important holy days, great crowds came to the temple early in the morning, bringing offerings of pineapple, coconut, and flowers.

Leaving the temple area, the Thaipusam participants march, run, dance, and shout through the streets for eight to twelve hours while a priest chants by their side. These men are fulfilling vows to their gods, or trying to earn a better place in the next life. Among others, we saw a seventy-eight year old man and a five-year-old boy with spears piercing their bodies as well.

Musicians and crowds follow, hoping to share in the holiness of the participants. They bow before them to be blessed, licking the sweat from their suffering bodies.

Making the little children kneel, they put a mixture of ashes and sweat scraped from the bodies of the dancers on their little tongues.

After dancing through the streets for hours, they return to the temple for the removal of the spears. We could see no sign of blood, of such great intensity is the demon possession. As one of these "holy men" walked away I looked for some sign of joy or victory on his face, but there was only a wild, vacant stare. I shall never forget his countenance oozing utter hopelessness. Oh, how the hope of Jesus is needed in this place!

LOST PARADISE
BALI

Bali is well known for its balmy breezes, waving palms, rolling waves, brown girls, orchids, and volcanic mountains. This little island in Indonesia, located just south of Java, fulfills all the romantic dreams that make up a South Sea island paradise. But it took us only three days to discover that the hospitable, smiling inhabitants of this tropical respite are bound by heathenism and superstition surpassing that of almost any other country we have visited.

Bali, a lost paradise in more ways than one

Bali Hinduism, the religion of the island, is a composite of Hinduism, Buddhism, Pantheism, Sun-Worship and several other ideologies. Every facet of Balinese life is wrapped up in their religion, and the people seem constantly occupied in preparing for some ceremony or ritual. If a man's behavior is good in this life, he has the chance of being reborn into a superior state in the next life; otherwise, he will reincarnate into a lower stage to begin again the progressive march toward perfection. An evil man is punished by being reborn into a dog, snake or a worm.

If an individual has attained the greatest wisdom, and has reached the highest position among men—that of a Brahman who has been ordained as a priest—he hopes to obtain liberation from this cycle of births and become a god.

En route to a cremation ceremony, our guide told us that in the history of Hinduism, he knew of only seven men who had attained to this degree of perfection. They had disappeared into Nirvana—or "Nothingness"— never to be heard from again. Then he proceeded to tell us of an experience he had:

> *"Each night before I sleep, I sit on my bed in a yoga-like position and concentrate on the middle of my forehead between my eyes. One night, I felt my soul being pulled from my body, and my soul began to float away. Then I became afraid and woke up."*

Evidently, our guide had not quite attained the degree of perfection necessary to reach Nirvana.

We listened to our guide explain how the locals believe that cremation, or burning of the dead, is not an occasion for mourning, but rather for celebration. Burning the body liberates the soul of the dead from this life so it can attain to higher things in the next life to be free for reincarnation. Failure to liberate the soul by neglecting to perform the cremation would force the soul to turn into a ghost that would haunt the descendants.

The explanation of the ceremony we were about to see was interrupted by a noisy procession of people letting off fireworks as they played music and marched. I attempted to get a picture of this frenzied mob, but quickly dashed to the shelter of the car for fear of being trampled!

The tall cremation tower, carried aloft by several hundred men, was built of wood and bamboo. At the site of the cremation, two wooden bulls, one red and one black, representing Brahma (the Creator) and Vishnu (the Preserver) were put in the tower. The white bull Siwa (the Destroyer) is kept at the home of the priest.

After slits were cut in the bulls and the top of the cremation tower was removed, the bone effigy—or likeness of the deceased—was placed inside. On occasion, the body is cremated immediately after death, but in most cases the family cannot meet the financial demands of the cremation ceremony, so the corpse is buried. In this case, the man had been buried ten years, and only a few bones could be found.

Following the bones, which were wrapped carefully in sheets, beautiful offerings of fruit, silver, batik cloth and all types of food were put in the bull's stomach. These offerings were to accompany him on his journey. Nothing was forgotten, as even a mirror and comb were provided so the deceased could comb his hair in the next life!

All of this was then sprinkled with holy water from eight different temples, covered with the "lid," and then set on fire. During this time the widow stood near the bulls with a colorful bird of paradise, supposedly leading the way to eternal life.

During the burning, I noticed several small boys with a chicken, which they released as smoke and fire ascended into the air. I was told that any evil spirit that might have attached itself to the body was thus released through this hapless little bird.

That evening after returning to the hotel, we heard the tinkling of the gamelan orchestra. Here were our friends of the afternoon, with offerings for the sea and an effigy, or likeness, of the deceased made from his ashes. The ashes and offerings of fruit, rice and cakes were given to the sea.

Thus ended the cremation ceremony. The man's soul had been liberated through the elements of purification—earth, fire and water—and he could now continue on his journey.

The next day, we attended a pantomime in a nearby village. This pantomime, known as the Barong, symbolized the struggle between good and evil.

Approaching the village, we could already hear the music of the gamelan orchestra. Balinese music is like bells interwoven with the fast humming of the cymbals and punctuated here and there by booming gongs, the whole controlled by the two drummers who beat unusual rhythms on the heads of their drums, each differently tuned. All of the pieces accompanying the Barong were masterpieces of musical structure and readily acceptable to Western ears.

In the play, which lasted almost two hours, the female witch, Rangda, has a contender for supremacy in a fantastic animal, a mythical "lion" called Barong. Because of an ancient feud with Rangda, he sides with human beings to thwart her evil plans and the Balinese say that without his help, humanity would be destroyed. Rangda is the night, the darkness from which emanates illness and death. The Barong is the sun, the light, medicine and antidote for evil. In the end of the pantomime, evil wins out, so the followers of the "good" spirit Barong proceed to stab themselves with spears or krisses.

In preparation for the play, the followers of Barong—a group of half-naked men—have visited the temple, where the priest has consecrated some water and sprinkled it on them causing them to shake all over as if in an epileptic fit. In a trance, they get up drawing their krisses and advance toward the witch. The spell is so strong that even though they push the sharp points of the daggers with all their might against their naked chests, they are not hurt and there is no blood. Some leaped wildly or rolled in the dust, pressing the krisses against their breasts and crying like children, tears streaming from their eyes.

The dance can only be performed with impunity under complete trance; otherwise, a man will wound himself or hurt others. Possessed as they are, they have supernatural strength and it takes many men to hold them down. Even after the kris has been wrenched away, they continue to dance with a blank stare and with the right fist still clenched as if grasping the kris handle. To take the men out of the trance, they were led one by one to where the Barong stood. The priest wiped the face of each man with the beard of the Barong dipped in holy water and gradually the hysterical men came out of their trances, dazed, simply walking away as if they did not know what had happened to them.

Even in the heat of the midday sun, we could sense the dense darkness in this symbolism of man's search for truth.

We left Bali the next morning, awed once again by the view from our plane window, but with sadness that there were still so many who had not yet come to knowledge of the truth.

ONLY A BARBED WIRE FENCE
HONG KONG

Bright sunlight filtered through the window of our Boeing 707. Below, was the sprawling city of Los Angeles. It was Easter Sunday morning. More than two years had passed since we left the snow-bound New England coast on a safari that had taken us around the world.

After leaving Tokyo on Friday, the 13th, with the accompanying ill fortune of an 8-hour layover in the Tokyo airport, we crossed the International Date Line. This necessitated our having to live through another Friday, the 13th, but we survived without event.

1962—Missionary Peggy Thornton and I in Hong Kong

Our journey was ended, but our hearts still thrilled as we thought of our last overseas crusade in the once British crown colony of Hong Kong.

In order to get to our service at New Life Temple each night, we crossed by ferry the mile-wide harbor that separates the peninsula of Kowloon from Hong Kong. On either side, the hills and mountains stand like gigantic sentinels. The intervening stretch of water is constantly studded with vessels of every conceivable size, from warships of the nations and majestic liners, to ubiquitous junks and sampans. A bustling, clamorous life prevails as steam launches dart hither and thither. Innumerable sampans wriggle their courses backwards and forwards between ship and shore; junks, with their sails of varied patterns, pick their way up and down the fairways; ocean-going steamers move in stately fashion to and from their moorings.

New Life Temple overlooks this busy waterfront. Each night its neon lights beckoned coolies in their light blue garb, young ladies in cheongsams, old ladies in black silk hanfus, their tight pigtails pulling their wrinkled skin taut, wealthy businessmen in tailored suits, and the occasional lonesome sailor to the meetings.

These dear people had such faith! We shall never forget the look of ecstatic joy on the face of the mother when her little boy heard for the first time in his life, and repeated, "mama," or the crippled boy who walked immediately after prayer. The last Friday night of the campaign, God visited the temple in a remarkable way. Waves of glory swept through the building. Many young people received glorious Pentecostal experiences while many others were divinely renewed.

Just a few miles from the harbor was an even narrower

stretch of water and a barbed wire fence. This gnarled fence explained the heartache in every Chinese breast. It separated free China from Communist Red China; wife from husband; brother from sister; children from parents.

Between 1948 and our visit in 1962, more than a million refugees from hunger-ridden Red China had crossed this border into the tiny British colony, swelling Hong Kong's population to nearly 3.5 million at the time. These refugees endured the most incredible hardships in their flight by land over rough, ravine-laced terrain or by sea, crammed below the decks of smuggler junks. Many were caught by border patrols of police and gurkha soldiers as they hid in the underbrush-covered hills.

A missionary pastor wrote this description:

> "Through a thin bamboo wall, I have heard the racking sob of a suffering giant. Here, on the edge of the night, one is acutely aware that the shadow of the hammer and sickle falls across our world. Minutes away, more than five hundred million human beings live in virtual slavery."

Bob and I made the journey to the border, where we looked across and saw the marching red guards prancing back and forth in front of the barbed wire fence that seemed to say.

"Satan has won a victory. He has sealed off this vast area with its more than 500 million souls. Preacher, you can't cross this barbed wire. The door has been closed and these people are without Gospel light."

Something rose up in Bob's spirit as we were praying over this country, and I remember him pointing to the barbed wire fence and saying,

"Satan you're a liar. You have no ability to close any door. Our God has declared that He will build His Church, and even the gates of Hell will not stop it. We proclaim victory and freedom some way, somehow for the lost of China."

But observing how communism was spreading like a raging fire across Asia and other parts of the world, we realized that even though we were on our way back to the United States, it would not be for long. We knew in our hearts we would have to return and preach everywhere there was an open door and an opportunity to proclaim the Gospel.

HONG KONG, HAWAII AND HOME

From Hong Kong, we returned to the U.S. via Hawaii

for a second honeymoon. What better place for rest and relaxation after more than 2 years of non-stop travel and ministry than this paradise?

After our Hawaiian holiday, we returned home, living through two of the same Friday, the 13th, on our inbound flight to Los Angeles. But it wasn't long before we were planning and preparing for our next missionary trip, which would take us to Latin America.

We were overjoyed to welcome our first-born son, David Shawn, on April 24, 1963, born in Long Beach, California. When he was three months old, we departed for Latin America.

Conducting open air meetings
in Latin America

CHAPTER 4
Latin America

BRITISH GUYANA, 1963

Bob first visited British Guyana at the age of 18, after feeling the Holy Spirit leading him into missionary evangelism and specifically instructing him to go to British Guyana.

At the time God spoke to Bob, he was attending a missionary conference with a dear pastor friend, J.R. Cisna in Tulsa, Oklahoma. As Bob shared what God was speaking into his heart, Pastor J.R. was astonished. Only a few months prior, an interesting couple had appeared in his church. They were a Chinese family—living in British Guyana—who had an experience in Pentecostal Baptism with speaking in tongues. They were unsure what was happening, but had heard that there were people in Tulsa who could explain to them what was taking place. This couple—the Chous—traveled to Tulsa, attended Cisna's church, and Cisna had their contact back in Georgetown, British Guyana. Hurriedly J.R. and Bob composed a letter in which Bob offered to come and conduct a nationwide crusade, as that is what God had told him he should do.

The Chous responded that they had been praying for such to happen and would be happy to do whatever they could to cooperate. Over the next several days, Pastor J.R.'s son-in-law, John Broxson and his new bride, Chris, felt led of God to join the crusade the three traveled as a team to Guyana. In obedience to their calling, the little evangelistic team departed within a few weeks. Bob did not feel comfortable sharing with the Broxsons that he only had $5.68 in his pocket!

The small group of believers, who had been praying for revival, met them at the airport. Per Bob's request, they had rented an auditorium, printed 100,000 flyers and bought newspaper and radio advertising. When he stepped foot out of the airplane, Bob found that he was in debt thousands of dollars in a land where the average man's wage was about $12 per month.

But God honored faith and obedience by sending revival and manifesting His power in miracles of healing. During the following weeks, thousands of people made professions of faith in Christ as Savior and were taught the responsibilities of stewardship. As a result, every expense of the crusade was covered, with enough left over to start a building fund to construct a church for the new converts.

This group of believers gathered a love offering for the young evangelists, which enabled Bob to visit and preach throughout South America.

When Bob arrived back in the United States, he had a $5 bill in his pocket. The entire missionary journey had cost him a total of 68 cents! The Guyana crusade launched Bob on a career of world missions that has spanned nearly six decades.

Fast-forward to 1963, and you find Bob and myself winging our way to Georgetown, British Guyana, with a brand new baby boy in tow.

Once again, there was great receptivity to the Gospel message with large crowds, many conversions, and miracles of healing. The difference this time was that we worked with established churches that were able to teach and disciple the new believers beyond the initial event.

From Georgetown, we went to Surinam, Dutch Guiana. There was, and is, much devil worship and voodoo practice in that country. We soon discovered in a personal way that Satan is not happy when his territory is invaded. Bob's preaching was often interrupted by demonic activity. One woman, in a growling and very deep male voice, challenged the message. At the conclusion of the service, we prayed for her deliverance. After some moments, the devil in her finally gave up, but not without a fight. The following morning, she came to the missionary residence where we were staying. We barely recognized her as her dark countenance and mien had been replaced by peace and serenity.

A week later we were in Cayenne, the capital city of French Guiana. We had put baby David to bed in a dresser drawer with a mosquito net covering. That night, I was awakened with a blackness and oppression I had never felt before. The demon that had been cast out in Surinam was taunting me at the foot of my bed. The devil said, "You took my home. Now, I am going to attack your family." In spite of debilitating fear, I was able to reach over and awaken Bob. Together, we pled the blood. Finally, he left us.

We spent a year ministering in every South American country. However, during that time, David was sick with diarrhea and dysentery in each country we visited. When he was also plagued with altitude sickness in the mountains of Ecuador, we had to be retrieved by missionary plane and transported from Quito down to the coast. In spite of his illnesses, he was still referred to as "Gordito" (little chubby one.) This was probably due to the Coca Cola the doctors in South America prescribed in his bottle instead of milk!

YOUTH WITH A MISSION (YWAM) BAHAMAS, SUMMER 1964

After our year of crusades in Latin America with our constantly ill toddler, we made our way back to the U.S. to resume a series of crusades in churches across America. During that time, we were working closely with our good friend Loren Cunningham to help launch the first Youth With A Mission (YWAM) summer of witnessing that was to take place in the Caribbean. In addition to helping recruit the large team that Loren had envisioned, we spent most of the summer in the Bahamas helping to coordinate those first teams. Bob was the evangelist for the closing crusade in Nassau.

As it turned out, more than YWAM got launched that summer. Nine months later, Robert Dean Hoskins was born in Bangor, Maine! Soon after Rob's birth, Bob left for crusades in the South Pacific and went on around the world to lead an exploratory crusade in the city of Beirut, Lebanon.

For months, we had been nurturing a vision for the Muslim world of the Middle East, and we felt the best approach was to launch a crusade and see what doors God might open. Though many reported it to be the largest crusade in memory in Beirut, in comparison to other countries of the world where we had ministered, it was small.

Unbeknownst to us during this "little" crusade, Bob was making contacts that would lead to an invitation and a contract to produce a weekly television show to be broadcast out of Beirut, covering almost all of Lebanon and some of the neighboring countries.

He returned to the States full of excitement, and for the next few months we traveled sharing the vision and raising prayer support.

1965—The boys and I arriving
in Beirut

CHAPTER 4
Middle East Outreach

LEBANON, 1965

In 1964, while Bob was looking at a map of the world, the needs of the Arab-Muslim world gripped his heart. Simultaneously, he received a call from the Department of Foreign Missions asking if he would consider moving his family to Beirut, Lebanon, to establish a base for evangelism. This seemed to be a confirmation of his call. So, in November 1965, Bob and I, with our two small boys, David—a year and a half—and Rob—6 months— traveled to Beirut.

Bob had acquired a TV contract from the Lebanese government to air a weekly program. But after the release of just one episode, the Maronite Catholic bishop and the Muslim mufti expressed concern that if the program continued, it could start another holy war. The contract was canceled. What now?

After much prayer and soul-searching, Bob realized he had been called to the Middle East not to televise, but to evangelize. We would have to get creative in figuring out what method of evangelism would be successful in a land where it was forbidden to conduct large public gatherings.

As we lived and worked among the people, we realized that they had a great respect for anything printed. Islam is essentially the religion of "the book"—the Koran. "The book" was our answer to how to evangelize in this sensitive area.

We developed a simple six-lesson course in the Arabic language that started with the acceptable doctrine of Allah and ultimately led students to knowledge of Christ. When the book was ready, we advertised in a local Beirut newspaper offering free literature. Bob created some provocative ads with pictures of John Kennedy and Marilyn Monroe, and the response was immediate and big!

Due to the great response to the newspaper ad from Arabic-speaking countries, the Way to Life Correspondence School was launched. What started as file cards in a cardboard box grew to more than 400,000 students enrolled from 26 Arabic-speaking countries, with an average of 500 testimonies of conversion per month received in the Beirut office alone!

Simultaneously, the Way to Life radio ministry was started, beamed out of Addis Ababa in the Arabic language. As the work expanded, Phillip Hogan, then

Playing piano for Solid Rock concert

foreign missions director, suggested that the mission be called "The Middle East Outreach." It encompassed an evangelistic center in Beirut and a strong youth ministry under the direction of Bill and Esther llnisky. Brother and sister pair, Marwan and Mae Rifka, stepped into the role of leadership among youth.

So many young people attended the evangelistic center that the need arose to establish their own facility, known as Christ Chapel, located across the street from the American University of Beirut. We organized a group of students, who would often sit around and play instruments after chapel, into a contemporary Christian musical group we named the "Solid Rock." The Solid Rock put on concerts under the direction of Esther Ilnisky, which were exceptionally well-received. The group had invitations to sing not only on the American University campus, but also at the Hagazian College and Beirut College for Women. Though we sang and did not preach, per direction of the universities, these concerts turned out to be a real feeder into the evangelistic center in Beirut and drew many students to the coffee house ministry at Christ Chapel.

The Solid Rock concerts came to Beirut at just the right time. They grew in popularity due to the Jesus movement that was gaining momentum worldwide, as the ears of university students were attuned to Western contemporary music. These concerts were also a personal answer to prayer for me, as all my life I had been involved in music and felt my pianist gifts were not being utilized in the classical Arabic context. Some notable musical guests who appeared in concert with Solid Rock were Barry McGuire of "Eve of Destruction" and Tyrone Bragg, who played Judas in "Jesus Christ Superstar." Their music and testimonies were incredibly impactful.

During a concert at the Beirut College for Women, a

Piano teaching lessons in Beirut

Muslim girl named Lene accepted Christ as her Savior. She was given a Bible, which she proudly took home under her arm. Her enraged Muslim father forbade her to return to the chapel again and threatened to burn her Bible. She hid it under her mattress, but one day her father found and burned it.

Undaunted, Lene would call Mae Rifka at the office and have her read portions of Scripture over the phone. God saw her hungry heart. When Lene enrolled in a comparative religions class at the American University, the textbook required for the study of Christianity was...the BIBLE! Of course, her father was irate. "But, Baba, Baba," (term of endearment for father in Arabic) "it's required," she explained. So Lene got to study the Scriptures to her heart's content!

JOCKEY, SIZE 34

Living in a war-torn country could be unbearable but for some humorous incidents. I remember sitting midway down a church pew in Christ Chapel. Beside me sat George Assad, PhD. and president of our seminary, a distinguished man of serious mien. Missionary Bill Ilnisky was administering communion, thus it was a time of quiet meditation. As I glanced toward the foyer, I saw what appeared to be a holy man with a full black beard and clothed in a long white robe. He must have sensed that this was a religious gathering and apparently felt that he ought to cover his head. Reaching under his robe, he took off his shorts and perched them jauntily on his head. I would have thought this an apparition, had he not come in and sat directly in front of Dr. Assad and myself. When we looked up from our communion confession and meditation, we both saw a tag protruding from the holy man's "head covering" that proclaimed "Jockey, size 34." Needless to say, our pew must have shook as we tried to suppress our laughter.

MIDDLE EAST EVANGELICAL THEOLOGICAL SCHOOL

Desiring to train national leadership and to establish visible churches throughout the Middle East, Bob, along with a colleague, went to Baghdad, Iraq, to follow up with Way to Life students. They were both seized by secret police, along with 5000 file cards, and accused of being CIA spies.

They endured constant interrogation for 48 hours in a dank Iraqi prison, but were finally released and returned to the relative safety of Beirut. I remember Bob praying, "God, if you want to build a church in Iraq; You'll have to do it, because you won't find me back there." I know that was a good decision. A few days later ten people, including some Americans, were hung upside-down in the Baghdad square.

Bob decided that if he couldn't go to the students, he would bring them to Beirut. Miraculously, young men and

The Archbishop of Ninevah (far left)—one of our students at the Middle East School of Theology

women—including the Archbishop of Ninevah—came to the Bible School from all over the Arab world.

In the providence of God, George and Fatiyah Assad, orphans, who grew up and married in the Lillian Trasher Orphanage in Assiout, Egypt, came to Beirut. Receiving his doctorate from the Near East School of Theology, George Assad was highly qualified to direct the newly formed Middle East Evangelical Theological School. He and his family of 6 lived and worked with us until they were forced to leave the country in 1975.

On February 6, 1970, at the American University Hospital in Beirut, our family was blessed with an addition, this time a beautiful daughter, whom we named Kimberly Ann. The Arab doctor couldn't understand our delight at having a girl, since boys are so important in the Middle East. However, Kim was born to the cheers of *ID-hum-dill-lab* (Thank God) by the doctor and nursing staff.

NIGHT OF CAPTIVITY IN BEIRUT AIRPORT

As regional director of the Middle East, Bob often needed to travel to other countries to preach or attend meetings. My brother, David Crabtree, was to be the speaker for the missions directors' conference in Spain and I wished to attend, provided someone could take care of the children. Terry and Athena Rayburn, a newly married couple working with us in all aspects of the Middle East Outreach, agreed to move into our apartment for a few days and watch the kids. Since there was a lull in the fighting and childcare was covered, Bob and I left for Spain.

The next morning from Spain, we read in the newspaper that fighting had resumed in Beirut. Bob got through to Terry on the phone to check on the situation and let him know we had rescheduled the conference for Middle East missionaries, slated to take place in Beirut, to Jordan.

We made arrangements to move all of our missions personnel to Amman: the Abbott family; the Ilniskys; Joe and Edna Brown; ourselves; the Raburns; La Bries, and Bill Lyons. The Alia (Jordanian Air) flight from Beirut to Amman would leave the following evening. Bob relayed to Terry that the children's passports were in a safe in our bedroom with enough money to purchase the tickets. The Rayburns quickly packed enough clothes for a week and enough food for the rest of the day and headed to the airport with the kids in tow.

All seemed well until they arrived at the Beirut International Airport, which was a scene of total chaos. To quote Terry in his book, *Under the Guns of Beirut:*

> *"Ticket areas were already jammed. Luggage was piled in every nook and cranny of the passenger lounge. Mothers, with anxious eyes darting from side to side, patted the heads of their frightened children, while fathers made desperate efforts to buy tickets on any flight leaving Lebanon."*

The worst was yet to come. When Terry checked in at the Alia desk, the attendant scrutinized the children's' passports and pointed at the word CANCELED that had been stamped across each visa. Although the passports had not yet expired, the visas had been transferred to new passports, which were currently sitting somewhere among piles of paperwork at the American Embassy.

As it was Sunday, the embassy was closed. All of Terry's attempts to reach responsible personnel failed. The war had intensified, as signified by tires burning in the streets and news of increasingly violent kidnappings, killings and bombings. Terry persisted, trying every avenue to somehow get themselves and the children onto the next flight. Terry recounts that the Alia attendant was very helpful, but the Lebanese official remained cold and unbending:

"The children cannot leave the country without proper visas. It's the law! Even if they had visas they couldn't leave without one, or both parents," he said.

Terry goes on to describe the unfolding scene:

> *"Meanwhile, we watched out the airport window as an Alia flight came in. It filled with passengers and left. The realization that they would have to spend the night in the filthy airport with no food…(the children had consumed the sandwiches long before) produced different reactions.*

There was a painful moan from David. He was leaning against the wall past one of the guards, tears running down his face. Kiki (Kimberly) started crying, 'Stupid, stupid man.' Rob demonstrated the strangest reaction of all. He ran to the end of the hall, grabbed a metal trash basket and hurled it against the opposite wall. Before it could fall to the floor, he kicked it so hard it bent double around his foot. Waste paper bounced, flew and slid in every direction. Yanking his leg free, he waded through the rubbish, scattering it even more.

That night lasted an eternity. Kiki slept between Athena and me. David found someone who had a cake, talked him out of a piece and shared it with Robbie. It was a kind gesture for 4:00 in the morning."

Meanwhile, Bob had made contact with "the powers-that-be" at Alia, and was assured that I would be on an early morning flight the following day. Terry continues the saga:

"The explosions had stopped at dawn, so we went to the observation deck. Robbie yelled, 'It's an Alia plane. I saw it circle over the mountains. I think it's going to land!' We watched a few passengers deplane. But when the shuttle pulled away from the plane. No Bob or Hazel.

Every nerve plunged to rock bottom.

I heard my name on the public address with the instruction to go to customs. Rounding the corner, my heart jumped within me. There, standing next to the director, life-sized and in living color, was Hazel!

I hugged her neck and said, 'Stay right here. I'll be right back with your family.'

Hazel produced proof that she was indeed the children's mother, and took David, Robbie and Kiki through the exit. Athena and I presented our passports, which had never been questioned, and followed.

On the plane, I asked Hazel, 'Just how did you get into the airport without us seeing you?'

'It was the captain,' she answered. 'Alia started to cancel this flight because there were so few passengers, but the captain demanded to fly.' Tears tracked Hazel's cheeks as she sat with her sons on each side and her daughter on her lap. 'He radioed ahead and had a car waiting to take me straight to customs. He didn't allow anyone else off the plane until I was in the car.'"

In Jordan, the entire conference team met us at the hotel. Some of them had been up all night praying for us. There were a few tears, many hugs, and much thankfulness as we ate breakfast. Once again, God had brought us through a situation over which we had no control. He had protected and kept us. We were weary but safe; we had made it out of Beirut in one piece. In the services during the week, the Holy Spirit renewed our minds and bodies.

PEACE IN THE MIDST OF WAR

Although I had given my heart to Jesus when I was six years old, there was a sequence of events in my life that, in retrospect, were orchestrated events that really opened my eyes to the fact that Jesus loved and cared for me in a deep, specific, and *personal* way.

The first happened while we were home on furlough from Beirut, attending Christian Life Center in Long Beach, California. Wesley Steelberg, the pastor, asked me to play the organ for a special Monday evening service. Despite the hassle of needing to find a babysitter, I felt compelled to say yes to his request and play for the service.

I had never met the evening's special speaker, Dick Mills, before. After delivering his simple Bible study, he said, "I would like the lady in the blue dress that played the organ to stand. I feel directed of the Holy Spirit to give her some Scriptures on safety." Well, that lady in the blue dress was me! I carefully wrote down the Scriptures he relayed and put them into my Bible.

One year later, we found ourselves back in Beirut in the middle of the worst battle we had experienced during our tenure there. The Palestinian commandos battled the Lebanese army for days. Concerted efforts to negotiate had failed. This time, the fighting broke out near our apartment.

Our first floor apartment faced the sea, divided by a vulnerable wall of glass. Despite having lived many years in the midst of war, its impact was not lessened. When tanks rumbled by the main highway adjacent to our Beirut apartment and cannons exploded in a nearby refugee camp, I reacted immediately. I instructed David, 9, and Rob, 7, to huddle in the safest hideout in the house—the white enclosure of the bathroom.

With Kimberly in my arms, I raced into the interior bedroom, another shelter during attacks. "War, war, war . . . death and destruction all around us . . . will it never end?" I lamented.

Suddenly, I heard rockets shrieking though the air. The whistling sound signified that the battle was intensifying, which meant we were in serious danger and needed to get to the sanctuary of the basement quickly.

I carried Kim into the bathroom to get the boys and

Our family: circa 1970

reached for the blankets we kept at the ready for just such an event. Kim screamed in terror, but the complacency of the boys amazed me. They had lived with war so long that they seemed to think it unreal. I think that playing with their G.I. Joes® enabled them to transfer their fears; not realizing the battle going on outside the living room window was the real thing.

There was utter chaos in the basement shelter. Lebanese mothers were beating their breasts—arms crossed, palms smacking their collarbones over and over again—as they are prone to do when agitated. I fought to control my trembling as the heavens raged and the cannons sent their chilling message of destruction through the air. We sat on blankets we had spread on the floor, and slumped against the wall. "Dear God, give us peace . . ." I prayed.

Suddenly, the Scriptures that I had memorized as a child, the same Scriptures about safety that had been given to, "the lady in the blue dress that played the organ" a year ago at that special Monday evening service saturated my spirit:

> *"Thou shalt not be afraid for the terror by night; nor for the arrow that flieth by day." (Psalm 91:5)*

> *"A thousand shall fall at thy side and ten thousand at thy right hand, but they shall not come nigh thee." (Psalm 91:7)*

A supernatural peace poured over me and pervaded our blanketed corner. Kimberly stopped crying, sensing my serenity.

> *"The name of the Lord is a strong tower; the righteous runneth into it and is safe." (Proverbs 18:10)*

I watched as many of our neighbors continued to stream down the narrow stairs. An Arab man in his long white jalabiya descended, candle in hand. He seemed to float in the eerie atmosphere of the dark stairway, the candle flickering over his bearded, craggy face.

Suddenly, a Lebanese mother seated across the room, heavy with child and with two little ones beside her, became hysterical, her self-control shattered. I threw the blanket off my knees and hurried toward her. Clasping her hands gently, I began to pray: "Heavenly father! Help this, your child."

In a few moments, she became calm. She looked at me, her tear-stained face filled with gratitude and puzzlement. She squeezed my hand and settled against the wall in exhaustion. The serenity now spread through the makeshift shelter. Some fell asleep as quiet reigned.

As I sat there, I thanked God for Dick Mills' obedience to the Holy Spirit to give me those scriptures at the special service a year prior, and for God's faithfulness to allow them to be recalled to my mind for such a time as this.

What seemed an eternity later, daybreak brought with its light an intermittent quiet from the war noises. I rose from my cramped position, woke the children and crept cautiously upstairs. I could hear sheep bleating from the nearby hills, birds twittering and singing and crickets chirping. All seemed well, except for an occasional rifle crack.

We climbed some stairs to a balcony to try and assess the situation. I watched a refugee mother dressed in a long, black Burqa with her three children searching for shelter, furtive as animals. Suddenly, heavy mortar shells shattered the air and exploded in a nearby field. The refugees cowered against the building, gripped with fear. When the shelling stopped, they dashed for cover in a neighboring basement.

I stood there a moment longer before picking up Kimberly. "Come on boys," I said softly, and we walked back into the apartment.

LEAVING LEBANON
1975

During our years of residency in Beirut, we were constantly trying to survive the deteriorating political system, navigate strict curfews, and were forced to evacuate our home three different times. Most unsettling was that we were targets of an extremist terrorist organization that menacingly threatened me by telephone whenever Bob left the country.

Lebanon on fire

In late 1975, when the American government and the Department of Foreign Missions for the Assemblies of God requested that we leave the country for safety's sake, we made the hard decision to leave Lebanon. At this point, things had worsened to such a degree that we felt our American presence as missionaries was becoming a threat to the Lebanese Christians.

Around the same time, I got word that my mother was not expected to live much longer and that, if I wished to see her alive, I needed to go to her right away. I took 5-year-old Kim with me to say goodbye to her in the States while Bob and the boys stayed in Lebanon to pack and finish up.

When we arrived in Paris, the Herald Tribune—also known as "the missionaries' Bible"—reported that all hell had broken loose in Beirut.

I frantically tried every way I knew how to make contact with Bob. Unable to connect with him, Kim and I continued on to Des Moines, Iowa, to visit my mother and dad in their retirement facility. My brother, David Crabtree, along with his wife, Dawn, pastored a church in Des Moines as well.

The following two weeks were agonizing and the news from Beirut reported on television was horrific. Mission headquarters in Springfield, Missouri, had no information on Bob and the boys, so we had no way of knowing whether or not they were safe. Once again, God's peace enveloped us as we leaned on His promises and the church community that was praying for us.

Every time the phone rang, my heart skipped a beat. Finally, I answered a call from New York and heard Bob's voice on the line tell me, "The boys and I are fine. We're on our way to Des Moines." Once again, God had gone before us and made our way safe.

The boys enrolled in school there for six weeks, attending with their cousin, Beth. Bob, Kim, and I went on to San Jose, California, where my other brother, Charles, and wife, Ramona, pastored. We settled into a home in San Jose, enrolling the children in yet another new school and tried to find a new "normal."

It was an emotional rough patch for us as a family. Looking back, I am grateful that we were surrounded by wonderful family and the church at Bethel Temple during a time when we needed help binding up our wounds and walking through the healing process. We had lived through, then left, a very tense, war-torn situation; the children were having a hard time making cultural adjustments; I was dealing with the death of my mother; and Bob had to leave us shortly thereafter to return to the Middle East to officiate at the first-ever graduation of the Middle East Evangelical Theological School following moving the school to Egypt. He also had important loose ends to tie up in Beirut.

One morning shortly after Bob had left, I vividly remember standing at the kitchen sink around 10 a.m.

David gazing over Sidon

washing dishes. I was overwhelmed with a burden for Bob, so I went upstairs to our bedroom, threw myself on the bed, and wept and prayed for over an hour until the burden lifted.

When Bob returned on Christmas Eve, during our drive home from the San Francisco airport he began to recount all that had happened since I had seen him last.

Here in Bob's own words is the gripping account of his return to Beirut:

"After getting Hazel and the children settled in a house and enrolled in school in San Jose, I had to make a trip back to the Middle East. We had moved the Middle East Evangelical Theological School (MEETS) from Lebanon to Egypt because the school could not function in the Lebanese civil war environment. Since it would be the first graduation after establishing the school in Egypt, I felt that it was important that I be present. Dr. Robert Ashcroft was the keynote speaker for the ceremony.

My first stop was in Beirut to check things out there. I was happy to find everything intact at our apartment. I accomplished a lot since there was a real lull in military activity before flying to Egypt to meet up with Dr. Ashcroft.

We enjoyed an incredible time with the Bible School students and graduated a large class. After the ceremony, I finalized some details at the Lillian Trasher Orphanage and booked my flight back to Beirut.

While I was in Egypt, the military situation in Beirut had intensified, making it very difficult for me to find transportation from the airport to our apartment. The taxi driver who transported me demanded an exorbitant fee for his services upon arrival at our building.

After a heated discussion, we settled on a "fair" price. I was quite agitated over the exchange and may or may not have slammed the door on my way out of the taxi.

I ascended the stairs to the apartment I had left in good condition just a few days prior and found myself in a disconcertingly different scene than the one I had left.

There was a large padlock dangling from the doorknob, yet the door was slightly ajar. It appeared as if someone had broken into the apartment, then padlocked the door on the way out. It looked to me as if the apartment had then been forcefully entered yet again as the padlock had been smashed to gain entrance. Feeling anxious, I carefully crept into the apartment and found a total disaster. Not only had the apartment been trashed, but also almost all of the valuables had been removed.

All of a sudden, my eyes were drawn to the floor. I saw red bloodstains and my heart began to pound in my ears. I began to fear for the life of our housekeeper, Therese, who had been looking after the apartment. Searching the rooms, I found a note, which Therese had managed to leave taped to a kitchen cabinet.

"Mr. Hoskins, there are men trying to kill you. You need to leave the apartment immediately. Do not stay here—I fear they are watching the apartment for your return."

I was relieved that Therese had somehow been able to leave me the note, and hoped that perhaps she had made her escape and not been harmed during the break-ins.

Heeding her warning, I drove the lone remaining

mission vehicle to the apartment that had been occupied by fellow missionaries Bill and Esther Ilnisky. I was sure that their concierge would let me into the apartment.

When I arrived, I discovered that their housekeeper was there, and she was able to fill me in on the details of the situation. From what she knew, Therese had been staying with a friend when the attack on our apartment happened. Therese had recounted to her that she had been the one to discover the ransacked mess. A trustworthy source from our neighborhood told Therese they had witnessed the attack and warned her not to stay on the premises. This trusty neighbor also urged Therese to warn me not to remain in the apartment either.

The next morning, I began contacting people to discover exactly where Therese might be, and was relieved when I was finally able to make contact with her.

Since Therese had been identified as being connected to us, I was concerned that she was in great danger and ordered her to stay at the Ilnisky's apartment until further notice.

I was angry about the attack and the unfairness of the situation. There was one valuable item left in the apartment—Hazel's piano—which we had purchased at great sacrifice. I figured that whoever was observing the apartment would attempt to remove the piano at

some point, but in my anger I was determined that
I would beat them to it. I secured the help of some
Kurdish furniture movers, leased a truck, and got the
piano out of the apartment.

For the rest of the day, I took care of various errands
including going to the green line (the line that divided the
Muslim areas from the Christian) after dark to meet with
one of our church members. Since this member was on
the other side of the green line, I wanted to give him some
funds to help with the ongoing ministry there since I was
unsure when I would be able to return again.

I made my way back to the Ilnisky apartment. We
prepared a little food and decided that since it had been
such a difficult few days, we would retire early.

An hour later, all hell broke loose. We heard the rat-
a-tat of machine gun fire and bullets pinging against the
building. I dropped to the floor, then belly-crawled to a
window where I peeked out to get a view of the street. I
knew it was 7 p.m. because, as I went down to the floor,
I looked at my watch and noticed the time. I remember
thinking it was strange that I would be looking at my
watch, as if someone would ask me later what time I had
died… "well, it was seven o'clock," I could say. We realized
later that God was even in that detail, for it was 7 p.m.
in Beirut, which meant it was 10 a.m. in the morning in

San Jose where Hazel and the children were.

After reaching the window, I saw some automobiles that had been turned into military vehicles. Various groups would steal cars—they particularly loved station wagons—then cut the tops off and mount 50-caliber machine guns on the rear to create quite a deadly weapon.

There were two of these homemade "tanks" parked in the street, and men running around—some of them just shooting, it seemed, at random—raking the side of the building. I crept back to the living room and told the ladies that I was not sure what was happening, but I thought that we should get to a secure place. They went into the bathroom, where—if there is gunfire—your safest bet is to lay flat in the bathtub, which offers you some measure of protection. Each woman claimed a bathtub while I stole back to the window to see if I could determine more precisely what was happening.

I saw the men who were firing at the building start running toward the building itself, and perceived that they were getting ready to invade. At that point, I realized that we were probably the only people still staying in the building.

Trapped in the fifth floor apartment, I listened at the door to see if I could detect any activity on the stairwell. I heard the sounds of men climbing the stairwell and

Bob's car, riddled with bullet
holes, during the attack on
our Beirut apartment

had a strong premonition that they were coming for me. I
suddenly remembered that when we took the piano out of
our building, we brought it here to the Ilnisky building.
Therese had even warned me, "Mr. Hoskins, I fear that
there were people watching us, and now they know where
we are staying."

With that in mind, I realized that Therese had
probably been right, and that the people who were seeking
me were on their way up the stairs. I told the ladies that

the men were approaching and that they should lock themselves in the bathrooms and not open the doors under any circumstances.

I went to the door, where I anticipated meeting whoever was coming, and mentally prepared myself to try and negotiate with them if at all possible. If I could not negotiate, I would surrender myself to them so that the women would be left unharmed.

My muscles tensed as I heard footsteps coming closer and closer. Just when I thought they were at the door, there was a chaotic moment with much shouting and activity. I couldn't quite decipher what was happening, but instead of entering the apartment, it sounded like they were retreating back down the stairs.

Things quieted down for a few minutes until I heard footfalls advancing up the stairs again. At the same point that the previous crew had reached, there was another outburst of excited shouting and exclamations, followed by another mysterious retreat.

A third group made their way up the stairs, and then retreated in the same manner of the previous two attempts. After the third retreat, I waited until all was quiet, and crept back to the window to watch our would-be attackers getting back into their vehicles and speeding away.

Weak with relief, I told the ladies that something had

happened—I knew not what—but for some reason our attackers had left and that it appeared as if we were safe for the time being.

The next morning, I went downstairs to question the guard, who was not much of a guard at all for having allowed the armed men to enter the building. I asked him if he knew what had happened last night and if he knew who or what those men had been doing at the building?

He replied that they had come crashing into the building with their guns trained on him and demanded to know what floor I was on. In his fear, he had divulged my location.

He related that the gunmen began to ascend the stairs, and he estimated that they had gotten to around the third or fourth floor when he heard a large commotion and saw them come rushing back down. A few minutes later another group went up the stairs and—same thing— came scurrying back down. By the time the third group appeared, he summoned up the courage to ask them, "What are you doing? What are you looking for?"

Apparently they were very rude to him, telling him to "shut up" and that they knew what they were doing, ordering him to stay put. The bottom line was that he too had no explanation as to what thwarted the three groups of attackers and prompted their hasty departure.

The next day, I went to the American Embassy to try and obtain a visa to get Therese, who was from the Seychelles and not a Lebanese resident, out of the country because I feared for her life.

The Consulate, understanding the situation, said he would help me get the visa for her, but that I should also get out of the country as soon as possible. Word on the street was that one of the most vicious commando groups was out to take my life. The Consulate would expedite the visa, we could come and get it tomorrow, and we needed to find a way to get out of the country ASAP.

Since there were no scheduled flights going to Europe, the only way out of the country was a once-a-day Air Jordan flight to Amman. Through my friendship with people within the Jordanian Airlines organization, I was able to secure tickets on the flight for Therese and myself. Once I went back to the Embassy and obtained her visa, the Consulate again urged me to take that flight and leave as quickly as I could.

Therese and I flew to Amman, transferred to a flight from Jordan to Europe, then winged our way to San Jose arriving on Christmas Eve night.

It was there, as I shared my account with Hazel, that we discovered it was at the very same hour the men were attacking us in the Ilnisky building that she had stopped *scrubbing dishes and was interceding and pleading for my life.*

Dr. Ashcroft called after he learned that I was back in the States to inquire about how things had gone during my return to Beirut. When I related the account to him, there was a long pause before he said, "I believe it's very possible that angels about nine or ten feet tall were poised on that third floor landing, and perhaps they confronted the commandos with flaming swords and sent them in fear back down the stairs."

Perhaps I will never know until Eternity what really occurred that night, but I am ready to accept Dr. Ashcroft's idea and give thanks to God that the angels of the Lord do encamp around about those who fear Him!

LESSONS FROM LEBANON

I learned two very valuable lessons through the Lebanon experience. Firstly, the value of intercessory prayer. If God burdens you to pray for someone, stop whatever you're doing to pray for that person. It can mean the difference between life and death.

Secondly, I learned that "things" aren't that important. If you have "things," thank God for them and don't let "things" have you. Someone once famously said, "Don't sweat the small stuff." In the light of eternity, it's all small stuff. The only thing salvaged in this world will be God's Word and the souls of men.

In my newsletter, entitled "Coffee with Hazel," I wrote to our friends and partners to let them know we were safe and of our change in venue.

David and I getting
Rob fixed up!

Coffee with Hazel
Des Moines, IA, Oct 1975

*How can I ever convey to you, my dear friends, the
gamut of emotions we have recently experienced as
Lebanon has been rocked by civil strife?*

***Fear** as guns, mortars and rockets, have exploded
around us, armed men appearing at our door
demanding money for their cause.*

***Sadness** for thousands of the bereaved, who have
lost family and friends. And for a beautiful nation self-
destructing physically and economically.*

***Relief** when the fighting subsides and we can get food
and rest.*

***Thanksgiving** for the Shepherd who lovingly cares
for His sheep, who "leads beside the still waters," who
"prepareth a table," who protects.*

*I'm sure you have seen the extent of destruction in
Lebanon on TV and in the newspapers, so I'll not burden
or depress you with further details. We personally feel since
no concessions have been made on either side, we can
expect intermittent fighting throughout the year until the
spring elections.*

Still, we are not quitting! Merely rearranging our

"home base" and intensifying the activities of Middle
East outreach.

Due to heavy fighting near the Middle East Evangelical
Theological School, Bob quickly moved our students, along
with Dean George Assad, wife and five children, to the
Lillian Trasher Orphanage in Assiout, Egypt. He will
return to Egypt to move the school to the Assemblies of God
properties in Port Said.

We have received very little mail during the last
months, due to the virtual shutdown of the postal
services. If the civil strife continues in Lebanon, pray
that God will lead us to a neutral country that will
serve the rest of the Arab countries and North Africa.

This is the second time during our ten-year tenure
in Lebanon that we have been forced to evacuate the
country: first during the 1967 Arab-Israeli war and
secondly this past week. Each time we have left with
a suitcase each, not knowing if we will ever be able to
return. More meaningful than ever is the statement, "The
only things that will be salvaged from this world are souls
and His Word."

Pray for our three children: David, 12; Robbie; 10; and
Kimberly, 5, as they attempt to adjust to a new culture,
environment, and school. Pray for Bob as he returns to the
Middle East, that God will help him in the many decisions

he must make under very difficult conditions. We would love to hear from you at our Des Moines address.

- Hazel

It was nice in Nice

CHAPTER 5
Vive La France!

NICE, 1976

After returning to the States, we had a huge decision to make. We had carried so many leadership responsibilities for the Middle East, yet we still did not feel fully released from the burden of its people. Heretofore, Beirut had been an island in the Arab-Muslim world from which to minister. Where were we to go now?

After much prayer, we decided to move to Nice, in the south of France. From there, Bob would still be accessible to his areas of leadership: North Africa, the Middle East, and Greece.

Living in France proved a peaceful transition for the children and me, although we were often lonely with Bob traveling so much between the Middle East and the United States. The summer we arrived, Kim quickly picked up French, playing with newfound friends in our apartment building. In the fall, she opted to attend the French Public School with *ses amies* (her friends.) I would drop her off at school and then proceed down the hill to the

International School where the boys attended and made life-long friends; namely, the Synkarski twins—Peter and Nick—from South Africa. After depositing David and Rob, I would then make my way to the University of Nice where I studied the language each day.

I discovered the French were kind about age. One is never "old," rather, *d'un certain age* (of a certain age). Going around the class, we were to specify which age group we were in. I said, *"Madame, Je suis d'un moyen age,"* meaning to say I was middle-aged. Instead, I had said, "I am from the Middle Ages!" My teacher replied, rightfully so, *"Oh, Hazelle, c'est pas possible,"* (it's not possible.) I should have said, *"Je suis d'un AGE MOYEN"*...adjective AFTER the noun.

Knowing French helped us to adapt to the culture more easily. Of course, the cuisine was not hard to take! David visited a farm and learned how to make foie gras—a disgusting process with incredible results! It still remains one of Bob's favorite dishes.

Against my wishes, Bob decided to succumb to the boys' pleas and get them mopeds saying, "It will help you, Hazel, so you won't have to transport them to school each morning." Right! Not too long after the acquisition of wheels for the boys, we got a call from the hospital. Rob had run into a van. Not just any van, it was unfortunately a vehicle of the gendarme (police!) The injuries, fortunately, were not life threatening, and perhaps the accident helped the boys be more careful in the future.

We made many life-long friendships and God-ordained contacts during our time in Nice that have ended up furthering our ministry, even to this day.

Bob accepting the leadership
of Life Publishers

CHAPTER 6
Life Publishers

❧

FLORIDA, 1980

After working out of France and fulfilling our responsibilities across the Middle East and North Africa, we began to feel that God was leading us in a different direction. In 1979, Phil Hogan, Director of Missions for the Assemblies of God, asked Bob if he would consider taking over the Spanish Editorial Vida ministry located in Miami, Florida, and expanding it into an international publishing entity. The new ministry would be designated Life Publishers. After much prayer and heart-searching, we felt that this was God's will for us.

In August of 1980, we moved to South Florida. We enrolled the children at Westminster Academy in Fort Lauderdale and found a haven in Oakland Park Assembly of God (now Christian Life Center) pastored by Max and Ophelia Yeary. I enjoyed playing the piano there for almost thirteen years, watching the children become involved in youth activities, and basking in a community of believers, as we established friendships that still continue to this day.

God poured His favor out on Life Publishers as the ministry experienced rapid expansion. Over the next years, it became one of the foremost publishers and distributors of Bibles, curriculum and other Christian materials in major languages—primarily Spanish, French and Portuguese. Study Bibles were developed specifically for children, youth and women.

One of the most aggressive projects was the translation of the NIV version of the Bible into Spanish (*Nueva Version Internacional*). That translation now blesses the entire Spanish-speaking world. Perhaps even more exciting was the development of the *Full Life Study Bible*. A missionary theologian from Brazil, Don Stamps, approached Bob asking if he would publish a set of Pentecostal study notes, which Don had authored, for the Church in Brazil in Portuguese. As Don and Bob looked over the project, they felt the leading of the Lord to put the notes into a new study Bible. Over the next months, Don worked with leading Pentecostal theologians and the result was what is today known across the world as the *Fire Bible*, originally called the *Full Life Study Bible*. Today it is the most widely translated study Bible in the world!

During this stage of our lives, watching our children

grow and thrive in the Word, Bob became more and more burdened for ministry to children. A big change was about to take place—a new day and a new year, with hope for us all.

A NEW YEAR

Being a doting grandmother myself, I love "grandmother" stories. Kids are so genuine and unaffected. Some time ago, I heard the story of a little boy who was visiting his grandmother in Minnesota. He fell asleep to gentle snowflakes and awoke to a winter wonderland. As Grandma looked out the window at the freshly fallen snow and the sun glistening on the icicles, she exclaimed:

> *"Didn't God create a beautiful world?"*
> *The little boy replied, "and He did it all with His left hand!"*
> *"Why do you say that?" asked Grandma.*
> *"Because JESUS IS SITTING ON HIS RIGHT HAND!" replied the boy.*

On New Year's Day, 1980, during our time of furlough and fund-raising in Montana, I penned the following lines. It was an idyllic morning, after a freshly-fallen snow.

GOD'S PERFECT WORLD: A PRAYER FOR THE NEW YEAR

Lord, what a perfect world You've made,

With icicles transparent, pure:

Hanging like stalactites

From the window there.

Majestic elk towering against a moonlit sky;

Timid deer darting nervously across the road;

Their fluffy tails bobbing

Like balls of cotton.

I don't blame you, little fawn,

Man scares me, too;

With his bombing, killings,

Abortions, rapes.

At times I want to run...

Adam and Eve lived in their garden.

Their perfect world you made;

But sin reared his ugly head,

Destroying paradise;

From your heaven you did come,

The sinless, spotless Lamb:

To wash and make things new again,

To fulfill redemption's plan.

This morning as I trek your prefect world,

With sun glistening like diamonds on new-fallen snow;

Cleanse my heart,

Make it transparent, pure;

As I face this new day, this New Year;

Trackless, untried,

In man's imperfect world.

January 1, 1980

ON HOPE

"Why art thou cast down, O my soul? and why art thou disquieted in me? HOPE thou in God; for I shall yet praise Him for the help of His countenance." (Psalm 42:5)

I had been so discouraged, and felt this Scripture—given as an interpretation to a message in tongues—was just for me! As I entered the promise in my diary, I looked across the page to see a quotation from Khalil Gibran, a Lebanese philosopher, also on the subject of HOPE:

"I cannot say much about that which fills my heart and soul.
I feel like a seeded field in midwinter, and I know that spring
Is coming. My brooks will run and the little life that sleeps in me
will rise to the surface when called."

Growing up in the state of Maine, it was common for us to see the stark, frozen fields of winter. How we searched for the harbingers of spring: the first robin, the melting ice, and the first blossom that pushed its way through the frozen ground!

Perhaps you, too, sometimes feel that your life is like "the seeded field in midwinter." From all appearances, there is little hope and relief from the emptiness and boredom of everyday existence.

But take heart, my friend . . . spring has come. . . the time of the singing of the birds is here. The planted seed will bring forth harvest. HOPE thou in God.

Rob and Bob delivering the first
Books of Hope to El Salvador!

CHAPTER 7
Book of Hope

❧

FLORIDA, 1987

In 1987, during a time of fasting and prayer, Bob received another vision from God. The scenes that he described when he shared the vision with me was a Satanic attack—an attempt to literally destroy an entire generation. The targeting of young people and children for destruction was certainly more than distressing to this mother's heart.

After a time of fasting and prayer with our good friend and ministry partner, Dale Berkey, Bob felt God had spoken a specific direction into his heart. The message from God was, "I want you to take My Word to the children of the world, and you will do it through leaders." Since God had specified "His Word" and "leaders," the first step we took was to acquire the names of the fifty most powerful people in every Spanish-speaking nation—presidents, ministers of education, ministers of health—and to inscribe their names in gold on beautiful Vida Study

Bibles. We presented those Bibles to these leaders through missionary friends and our Life Publishers distributors.

As a result, we received invitations and were the guests of presidents in several countries. But most amazingly, an invitation came from the Minister of Education in the country of El Salvador, asking if we would provide the Word of God for every child in every school in the country. It didn't take a lot of discernment to understand that God was leading the way and showing us how we were to take His Word to the children of the world. The Vida team went to work to create a Scripture portion that would engage children and youth; the result was *El Libro de Vida,* which is now called the *Book of Hope.* Nearly a million children in El Salvador had God's Word placed in their hands in spite of the raging war.

In the ensuing years, the book would be translated into the many languages our ears had become accustomed to in our global travels, and would even make its way behind the Iron Curtain into the Soviet Union!

My first grandchild,
Diandra Hoskins

COME AS A CHILD

(Inspired by my first grandchild, Diandra)

I watched my grandchild today,
As with wonder and delight
Her eyes followed a scampering squirrel,
A bird flitting by the window.
Lord, don't let me become calloused and jaded
to the wonders of Your creation.
May I come as a child.

I watched my grandchild today,
As with tottering steps she made her way
Across the room.
Oh . . . she's fallen! But just as quickly up again,
Advancing with more courage and strength.
Lord, if I falter and fall, don't let me sit in my
weakness and self-pity,
But may I rise quickly;
For each time I try again, my steps grow stronger,
And I advance further.
May I come as a child.

I watched my grandchild today,
As with confidence she jumped into her daddy's arms
From a high place.
Lord, when the way is dark and I am afraid;
When the challenge is too great for me—
Let me leap into Your strong arms,
Knowing You will hold me.
May I come as a child.

June 10, 1990

Visiting the graveyard in Sarajevo

CHAPTER 9
Around the World with the Book of Hope

I could write volumes about my trips with Book of Hope, now OneHope, which has worked in 130 countries. But in the interest of saving trees, I will narrow it down to a few of the countries I experienced that especially impacted me.

BALKANS
SARAJEVO, 1997

We were driving from Zagreb to Sarajevo cramped in Pastor Felix's old Opel Kadett—hot and sticky from the Croatian sun. However, our discomfort was inconsequential compared to the horror unfolding before our eyes...

Each turn of the road brought new scenes portraying the aftermath of the war. Hardly a village had escaped shelling or mortar fire. Buildings that were still standing were completely derelict. Dwellings had been looted to the point that they resembled skeletons. Any walls that were still standing were peppered with bullet holes. We were devastatingly reminded of those who had died here.

We headed toward the mountain area where we would be stopping for lunch. The scenery changed drastically— from utter destruction to breathtaking beauty; tumbling waterfalls, crystal clear lakes with a turquoise hue, towering pines and silvery birches...a veritable Garden of Eden.

God, you created such a beautiful world. Then sin reared its ugly head with its evil and greed. Man destroyed your perfect world.

In Sarajevo, we felt dwarfed by the thousands of graves and white markers that dotted the hillsides. So many had been struck down in the prime of life and died in the raids.

Born: 1970　　　　　*Died: 1993*

The International Forces patrolled the streets; tanks enveloping fresh-faced 18- and 19-year-old boys keeping tenuous peace...so much hatred and desire for revenge still smoldering beneath the surface.

That night, with great fervor, the youth who were

meeting in a bombed out shelter sang:

"The name of the Lord is a strong tower—
The righteous run into it…and they are safe."

When the young people sang "the righteous run into it and they are safe"—they would run up to the front of the room and back to their seats again—the joy they had in the midst of such death and destruction was amazing to me. I will never forget those scenes.

RWANDA
KIGALI, 2003

By the flickering light of a candle, I could barely see the keys of the old, very out-of-tune piano. "Could we sing, 'I'd Rather Have Jesus?'" asked Jo Wilson. Her husband, Billy, was in the bush country doing evangelism.

We were in the home of veteran missionaries Murielle and Bob McCulley. Electricity was limited in Rwanda, thus the candle. Our voices rang out and what they lacked in tonality, they made up for in sincerity.

"I'd rather have Jesus than silver or gold
I'd rather be His than have riches untold"

Bob and I were with people who have spent their lives in Africa surviving malaria, war, and separation from family. Now here they were in Rwanda, encouraging a flourishing African church and training young people in the Bible School.

Rwanda, located in east-central Africa is a small, physically beautiful country with steep mountains, deep valleys, and the highest lake in Africa, Lake Kivu. Extending north of it are the Virunga mountains, which includes the occasionally-erupting volcano, Mount Karisimbi. Similarly, beneath Rwanda's apparent beauty smolders deep emotion, hurt and anger.

For 100 days, beginning in April 1994, the Hutu tribe rampaged through the country, slaughtering an estimated 1 million Tutsi and Hutu sympathizers. As in most civil conflicts, the genocide was brought on by a quest for power.

The church is a forerunner in the healing that is taking place among the Tutsi and Hutu tribes. In fact, the Assemblies of God Superintendent Garabazie—a Hutu— and his wife Christine—a Tutsi—are glowing testimonies of reconciliation. During the genocide, Christine fled to her family in Zaire. The newly married couple were separated for three years.

Another dynamic couple we met with a similar testimony were the Murigannes. Through contacts in the U.S., Rosette and her husband fled to Washington D.C. during the genocide. Mr. Muriganne taught at the prestigious Howard University there and the couple attended Assemblies of God church in Falls Church, Virginia, pastored by Richard Neubauer.

During a Sunday morning service, God spoke to Rosette's heart, "you must return home." Thinking God meant her home in Virginia, she began to gather up her things and make plans. "No, I mean you must return to Rwanda," God said.

Rosette and her husband obediently returned to the chaos of Rwanda, leaving the comfort and security of the United States behind. There, Rosette was especially burdened for the children who were orphaned during the genocide. She became a foster parent and was instrumental in finding homes for many children. God has honored this couple's obedience and sacrifice. During the time we were in Rwanda, Mr. Muriganne was the second in the government of Rwanda, a position equivalent to the Secretary of State in the United States.

"Than to be the King of a vast domain, and be held in sin's dread sway
I'd rather have Jesus than anything this world affords today"

The candle flickered and almost died. As we went out into the moonlit African night, we felt we had been in the presence of the King, as well as some of His choice servants.

RUSSIA
SEVERSK, 1992

My first trip to Russia was in 1992, traveling with a group of U.S. pastors and their wives. We arrived in Moscow at the Bible school after an 11-hour trip from JFK and a 4-hour layover in Helskinki. Toting our luggage up five flights, we discovered that our room for the night was a real prophet's chamber. Supper consisted of cold fish and sweet potatoes. We were so exhausted that we even appreciated the icy water of a cold shower to rinse us off before retiring gratefully onto our simple iron cots.

The next day, our group of 22, including five Russian translators, boarded a rickety bus and headed for Seversk, which means "to plant or sow seed" in Russian. We

Diandra and Bob at St. Basil's
in Moscow

were a high-spirited bunch, ready to conquer the world. Along the way, we took in the ravages of Communism: rust, decay, and half-finished buildings with peeling paint. By noon, we had broken into the stash of "junk food"— Cheez Whiz, crackers and Snickers bars—and consumed it with gusto. After a short pit stop—where else but in the forest!—we climbed back onto the bus, where a spirit of lethargy descended.

After travelling for nearly 9 hours, we finally arrived

in Seversk. It was raining and blowing dust. Our spirits dampened as we peered out the windows to see nothing but a grey, dingy building. We waited as one old lady wearing a babushka guided her chickens across the cobblestone streets. After many inquiries, we finally found our contact, a young Ukrainian missionary. He directed us to our "hotel." "Good!" we all thought, "I can't wait to take a hot shower!" Imagine our dismay when we discovered that the 22 of us were to share two bathrooms, and again, there was no hot water.

We assembled in a meeting room later that night for some more bad news. The young missionary, Sergei, had been unable to secure permission from the authorities to distribute the *Book of Hope.*

He suggested that we should spend the night, then return to Moscow the next day. Bob, to the astonishment of everybody, instead instructed the bus driver to leave and return for us the following week per the original plan! But what would we do for a full week, especially since the food and provisions promised were doubtful? After some discussion and prayer, we decided that Bob and two other men should pay a visit to the regional director—who had been appointed by President Yeltsin. The next morning,

Bob and the men visited the regional director's office while the rest of us stayed behind and prayed.

The director turned out to be a former communist boss, very grim and austere. After more than an hour of talking and trying to explain our mission, he was still refusing to help, telling us to leave the city. Suddenly, the door to the office burst open. Three men marched straight up to the director, who had jumped to his feet in astonishment. For five minutes they shouted into his face and then, without even acknowledging our presence, stormed out. The director turned to us and asked, "What do you need? We are pledged to help you in every way!"

It was only after he had agreed to arrange for a bathhouse for us, food, and every accommodation to enter the schools, as well as making the only auditorium in the city available for our meetings, that we had the courage to ask our translator Irene, "What happened? Who were those men?" Irene related that there had been a power struggle between that region and President Yeltsin, and that Yeltsin was trying to weaken the communist influence in Seversk. He had received word that the regional director had refused to accommodate the Book of Hope delegation, and had used it as an opportunity to exert his authority.

He had actually sent men from the government to Seversk to lambast the director and tell him in no uncertain terms he was to show the greatest of hospitality to the American team and to accommodate our every request. I can assure you that when Bob and Irene returned to the dilapidated building we were staying in with this report, there was a great time of rejoicing and thanksgiving to the God who has a way to open every door.

With the director's permission to distribute the *Book of Hope* in all the area schools, the mayor and minister of education, who had originally denied permission to distribute, joined in with enthusiasm. They even offered to provide a bus and accompany our group to all the schools in the region. The key to Seversk was ours!

The first school we visited was clean and orderly. The lady principal was a former communist. She took us to a room displaying medals and awards of the Young Pioneers and memorials of the war dead. We sensed that she wanted to concede to reconstruction, but was resistant to change. We found this to be the pervading sentiment, especially in the smaller, remote towns and villages where it is difficult for the older people to transition. Many have been entrenched in communism for the past seventy years with the state taking care of them, but now they are finding themselves caught in a vacuum.

The atmosphere warmed a bit when we engaged in questions and answers with the students. We distributed the *Book of Hope* to eighty students. As we left, I gave a pair of nylons to the principal. She kissed me on both cheeks as a tear trickled down her face. Compared to us, they have so little…

At the second school, a team member reported that an ex-communist, Russian-speaking teacher ventured a covert "God bless you" in English as an aside to him. The teacher then proceeded as if this episode had not occurred.

We wondered if the distribution in the two schools would affect our evening crusade at the Seversk Theater. We needn't have worried. The meeting was set to begin at 7 o'clock. By 6 p.m., the auditorium was jammed with people trying to get in. Our team members mustered up every ounce of creativity to occupy the crowd. They even dramatized stories from the *Book of Hope* to entertain the children in an overflow room upstairs.

We had learned a few simple choruses in Russian and the audience joined us in singing them with great enthusiasm. After another dramatization and songs from a visiting Ukrainian group, we did a simple Gospel presentation, then asked, "Would anyone like to accept Christ as Savior?"

Teenagers with tears streaming down their faces and children clutching the *Book of Hope* flocked to the altar. This scene was repeated during the two successive nights we held the meetings. Hundreds of decision cards were filled out, and we gave copies to the young Ukrainian pastors, Peter and Sergei. We agreed to send follow-up materials as well as visual Sunday school material to help disciple these new believers. By faith, they had already purchased a plot of land for their own church, and some of the pastors in our group agreed to supply the financial assistance for constructing a church building.

I was constantly reminded of Ephesians 1:12-14.

"That at that time ye were without Christ...having no hope, and without God in the world."

Russia and the CIS have been trapped in a spiritual vacuum fraught with atheistic teaching for more than 70 years. The young people are especially devoid of hope. Through the *Book of Hope,* we had been able to give them hope, the only Hope.

The morning of our departure, we were coming out of a restaurant onto the city square. An old lady was shuffling along with her chickens and a goat. Her wrinkled face reflected years of suffering and hardship. We gave her a *Book of Hope* and told her Jesus loved her. "But I don't feel His love," she responded. We prayed for her in front of a statue of Lenin. Under his stony stare, her heart melted with ours. Tears intermingled. She felt His love through us…His hand extended.

We had sown seed in Seversk; a church had been established; there was a harvest to be gathered.

MINSK
1993

In 1993, I led a team to Minsk, Belarus, Russia with Marty and Joyce Huff, resident missionaries with OneHope. Visiting a school for exceptional children was a memorable event. Friend, juggler and trumpeter, Lennart Persson, from the U.S. was on the team. We experienced music as a universal language when we joined in playing "O Sole Mio"—the only song we all knew!

On the morning before we left Minsk, I penned the following poem:

WEEP FOR MINSK

I awoke with heavy heart,
    realizing we're leaving our babes…
Our newborns in Christ,
    As sheep among wolves –
Wolves of greed, immorality and drunkenness.

God, will these lambs survive?
    Please send more laborers
To gather the harvest
    lest it be lost.

Send your mighty men –
    Men of velvet steel,
Who will laugh at impossibility,
    see visions, dream dreams;
Shepherds who will gather the little ones in their arms
    And love with tenderness,
To show the fathers of Minsk the way;
    That strength is not in muscle and brawn,
But in gentleness and sound mind.

God, help the women
    Who, with stooped shoulders and gnarled hands,
Care for the victims of Chernobyl
    and with meager means work night and day
To set a table for the children
    and the husbands who abuse them
        physically, emotionally, spiritually.

God, as you wept over Jerusalem
    Weep for Minsk
Suffer the little children to come unto You,
    And forbid them not,
For of such is the kingdom of heaven.

November 2, 1993

CHINA
BEIJING, 2006

In the past decade, we've witnessed the most incredible manifestation of God's grace across China. My first trip behind the "Bamboo Curtain" was in September of 2006.

It was a thrill to arrive at our hotel and find the Chinese leather Leader's Edition of the *Book of Hope* awaiting us! This was printed in diglot form where Mandarin and English were side by side on the pages. The best part? On the back cover was the ISBN number, which gave us permission from the government to publish and distribute!

When we showed it to the Chinese Christians, they could hardly believe it. "A miracle," they said. And indeed it was. After submitting the book to thirty-five publishers, the thirty-sixth received permission to publish. But instead of calling it the *Book of Hope*, they wanted to rename it, *The Life of Jesus*. We could live with that!

We spent many days shoulder to shoulder with various Christian groups designing the books for children. God sent us some very talented people, among them school teachers, publishers, and missionaries. They culturally adapted the books, as well as determined the heart-felt needs of Chinese children and young people so that we could customize the programs we were developing.

We had a chance to do the usual tourist things: visiting the Temple of Heaven, Tiananmen Square, the Forbidden City and the Great Wall of China—a great feat when you realize it took hundreds of thousands of workers 10 years to construct. One hundred million cubic meters of rammed earth were used to form the core of the original wall.

As we were worshiping with about one hundred people in a Chinese house church, the Chinese Christians raised their hands to heaven and prayed fervently with tears streaming down their cheeks. I thought of all the sights and sounds we had seen and heard the previous week, but this was the most impactful. The Great Wall is made up of rocks and stones—inanimate objects—but that morning I was reminded of 1 Peter 2:5, which states, "You also, like living stones, are being built into a spiritual house."

Restricted so far as worshiping openly in a beautiful edifice, these believers had constructed a "spiritual house with lively stones." After Bob challenged them to distribute the *Book of Hope,* one young man said, "Too often we are cloistered here in this apartment. Although we will probably suffer persecution for our witness, we must go out beyond these four walls and spread the Gospel."

Distributing the 100 millionth
Book of Hope in Russial

CHAPTER 10
OneHope: Our Journey Revisited

As a woman from the "Middle Ages," my many years on this earth have afforded me the privilege and opportunity to return to countries where Bob and I planted seeds when we visited and started ministries years ago. Seeing the fruits of our labor has been one of the rewarding things about getting older. In our work with OneHope, we have been able to witness the growth and receive updates on the fruitfulness of the movements that God has blessed in each country along our journey. Here are a few accounts of some of the countries I have had the chance to revisit.

RUSSIA REVISITED

In September of 2000, we went to the city of Chita, Russia, to celebrate the 100 millionth distribution of the *Book of Hope*. After a more than 10-hour flight to Moscow, we boarded a charter plane with 80 Americans, along with the Russian choir from the New Testament Church in

Perm where Edward Grabovenko is the pastor. After seven more hours in the air, we arrived in Chita.

After ministry in Chita, we headed out for the town of Krasnokamensk, which is 332 miles southeast of Chita, near the Sino-Russian border. The rich uranium mines have caused this to become a "hidden city." Our first attempt to navigate the rough roads was cut short when a bus broke down. The next day, part of the team set out in several vans, only to again have some break down; however, a few of us soldiered on. One van contained a group from Alabama with Pastor Mike Rippy and members of his church. Another had the musician and artist, Travis Meadows, with Olga, the interpreter. Our van included Nicole Johansson, Bob and I, Dave Byker and the driver, who spoke only Russian. Dave sat up front with the driver, and "translated" for us in the back seat. It was quite a joke, as he spoke even less Russian than the rest of us. Halfway through the journey, we ran out of road and outhouses. ("OUT" of those bumpy vans beside a tree was much more refreshing anyway.)

Eventually, we crested a hill to see the lights of a large city stretched before us...Krasnokamensk, meaning "town on red stone." Our driver took us to a very dirty apartment inhabited by some very large cockroaches.

We were excited to find that an excellent job had been done advertising the concert. There was an overflow crowd that had come to see the Americans and hear our soloist, Travis Meadows. We had one small problem, however: Travis was held at the police station, due to a problem with his registrations! No amount of persuasion would convince the authorities that Travis was legit—not even seeing his picture on flyers all over town. But, as they say, the show must go on. We employed everyone on our team to perform…some good results, some not so much. Most every concert hall in Russia has a beautiful grand piano. Krasnokamensk was no exception, so I was able to put my musical services into action.

Fortunately, just when we were about to deplete our repertoire, Travis appeared! The response was overwhelming. The police had to be called to keep order and to prevent any more people from entering the auditorium. During the next few days, hundreds of young people heard the Gospel story for the first time, and expressed a desire to follow Him.

As we made the same arduous trek back to Chita, we asked Dave Byker what was the first thing he was going to do when he got back to the States. He replied, "Hug my toilet seat!" (This luxury was non-existent in our Krasnokamensk apartment.)

THE GOOD NEWS FOR RUSSIA!

Irene Litvinova, dubbed "the little general" due to her petite size, but largely capable of running an army, recently updated us on the ministry efforts we had begun in Russia.

She reported that the church in Chita that hosted the 100-millionth celebration planted a church in Krasnokamensk shortly after the distribution there.

In 2005, we launched teams who traveled by bus from village to village to help reach children and youth in small towns. The Chita church was the first to organize a full-time team working throughout the entire Chita region, the Republic of Buryatia and northern provinces of China to reach around 200,000 children and youth!

Thanks to the efforts of the American teams we led to Russia in the early years, we have been elated to watch the seeds that were sown and churches planted begin to grow and bear fruit. These early teams lead to the launching of *The Hosanna Plan*, founded on the vision of Pastor Edward Grabovenko, currently the head Bishop of the Pentecostal Union. *The Hosanna Plan* reaches people in remote places in Russia as well as plants new churches in areas where there are none. Believers from all over the globe dedicate a year of their lives to travel as teams to the most remote and difficult regions in Russia. They live among the locals on meager means, and at great sacrifice, in order to expand the Kingdom of God. OneHope provides the critical evangelism resources needed to equip these teams as they go village to village sharing the Good News and planting churches. The goal of *The Hosanna Plan* is to plant 10,000 churches by the year 2020!

Often, the goal of mission is to work ourselves out of a job. Such is the case in Russia. Those that speak the language and are part of the culture can often be much more effective than an outsider coming in.

In the fall of 2011, Bob and I attended a pastors' conference in Perm with several thousand pastors in attendance. When Bishop Edward asked how many came to Christ as a result of the ministry of OneHope, half the congregation raised their hands! Many had accepted Christ when the Americans came to their village with the little blue book—the *Book of Hope*. How rewarding is THAT?

CHINA REVISITED

"Everything is possible in China at some time; some place." This is a recurring phrase you hear from people who have lived and worked in the Chinese context.

Certainly in the visits we have made, we have had varying experiences. When we first visited, Bob preached in house churches brimming with ardent believers ready to put their lives on the line for their faith, many having endured prison or other consequences.

Today, it is very different. In one major city, we enjoyed visiting with the leaders of 87 churches totaling 200,000 believers—IN ONE CITY! Teachers from the area are constantly indicating that they want the materials we have to offer "yesterday!"

Our visit to Beijing in May 2013 was so encouraging. We now have the ISBN number from the government for the Chinese version of *The GodMan* film with the accompanying book. We also have permission for another leader's edition of the *Book of Hope*. Church leaders are desperate for relevant Scripture materials for evangelizing and discipling children and youth, especially with the incursion of the Internet, X-rated films, etc. from the West. Through our research in three major regions, we now have multiple materials—both printed and digital—reaching tens of millions of children and youth annually.

INDONESIA REVISITED

We've had the opportunity to return to Indonesia a number of times since those original crusades in 1962. Once again, it is amazing to see how God is building His Church, even in a country noted as having the largest Muslim population in the world.

Today, when we visit, I get to "sit there" as Bob preaches in great churches to thousands of believers; we witness strong missions programs reaching out, not only to Indonesia, but also beyond. In spite of the challenges of evangelism in a Muslim context, the OneHope ministry in Indonesia has seen unbelievable doors of opportunity open to give the *Book of Hope* to schoolchildren in government-run schools.

The testimonies of miraculous conversions, coupled with the testimonies of those who have suffered incredible persecution once they testified to their faith, could fill an entire book! God's Word is having incredible impact in Muslim countries where persecution often comes from a person's own family, as apparent in Tumine's* story.

Tumine comes from a part-Javanese part-Maudrese family, where her father is a devout and influential leader of a fanatic Muslim organization. After reading a copy of the *Book of Hope,* Tumine made a decision for Christ. When she shared this with her mother, her mom begged her to reconsider her decision and told Tumine that she must quit her job, return home, and become Muslim again. But Tumine was granted such a strong faith that she walked away from her family, got baptized, and began to be discipled by her pastor. Tumine has been told that she may never come back home unless she would relinquish her faith in Christ and return to the Muslim faith.

BURMA REVISITED

During our first visit to the country of Burma, we produced a short film called "On the Road to Mandalay" and had the opportunity not only to conduct crusades in the capital of Rangoon, but also in Mandalay.

Burma, known today as Myanmar, has gone through rough years of repressive, tyrannical rule. The people have suffered in so many ways, and the Church especially has been confronted with persecution over those years.

However, it is now a new day in the old Burma. With the change of government and the new openness, opportunities abound for the spread of the Gospel. OneHope's ministry is now firmly planted, and some of the most rapid expansion in OneHope outreach is taking place in Myanmar. Working entirely through partnerships, teams are conducting research, translating and creating new projects, and stepping out in bold faith to reach the young people of their nation. Recently, some of our OneHope team returned to share this incredible story.

Lifen* grew up in a Buddhist family and had no knowledge of Jesus or the Bible. A friend invited her to go to a nearby village and listen to some stories. The stories were from our *God's Big Story* program and were so compelling to Lifen that, each week, this 10-year old girl walks an hour and a half each way to hear them. Lifen has given her heart to Jesus and has become one of the best Bible storytellers in the province. When she was asked what her favorite story in the Bible is, she responded, "Noah and the Flood. In the same way Noah saved his family, I want to save mine."

This is only the beginning of the fruit that will be borne in one of the newest OneHope outreaches.

INDIA REVISITED

Several years ago, Bob received an invitation from our good friend, Chuck Freeman, to join him and a group of Christian men who were doing a prayer conference in New Delhi, India. Bob was so busy with spreading the OneHope infrastructure around the world that his response to Chuck was, "Oh, India, it's a Hindu country and to take the *Book of Hope* there is going to be very difficult. I think I'll pass on the invitation." However after prayer, Bob felt he should go, and he joined Chuck on that prayer vigil.

Many of you have heard the story of how God miraculously gave direction and brought us into a relationship with the Pinto family, who have the largest private school system in the world in India. Through the relationship with Dr. Augustine and Madam Grace Pinto and their family, opportunities began to open for OneHope to reach India's children.

We rejoice today that in these intervening years, more than 100 million children and youth have received God's

Word. One of the greatest outreaches in OneHope history was the Hope India Campaign in which *The GodMan* film was telecast on national television simultaneously in thirteen languages and dialects. The Nielson type reporting for India reported that upwards of 500 million people saw *The GodMan*. It was exciting to hear that thousands of churches cooperated in the outreach by inviting children and youth into their churches and homes to view the TV showing, and to put a copy of God's Word in their hands. As I am writing this, more than 25 million children a year are receiving God's Word in India through OneHope programs. Oh, what great and mighty things God as done, and to Him be all glory!

Here is just one of many testimonies we have received from India.

Rebanta* was a Hindu. He followed all the religious rituals of his family, including worshiping idols. But despite walking many miles every year to visit the temple of Ayyappa (a famous Hindu God), he could not find peace in his life.

Rebanta attended a showing of *The GodMan*, after which he was given a copy of the *Book of Hope*. After reading the book, he came to realize that Jesus is the real God who gave

His life for him and is the only source of peace.

Rebanta faithfully attends the local discovery center to continue learning more about God's Word. Although his family does not believe as he does—they are one of the few who allow him to continue attending the discovery center in order to deepen his faith.

NEPAL REVISITED

In May of 2009, Bob and I returned to the mountain kingdom of Nepal. It was my first return since 1961, when the nation had initially opened to outsiders. We were able, at that time, to secure two of the first 50 visas issued to outsiders. The Nepalese looked at us as if we were from Mars, especially since hose with seams were in fashion! I guess they thought I was odd to have stripes up and down my legs.

We stayed in a mud hut, with no heat, and wrapped ourselves under layers of sheepskin at night trying to stay warm. It was a primitive and poor nation with virtually no Christians or churches. Following our return to the U.S. years earlier, we had shared the story of the sixteen Christians we had met with—the only ones in all of Nepal—and were able to get 868 people to sign a prayer card pledging to pray for open doors to Nepal. How God has answered prayer!

Today, there are hundreds of churches, many of whom now partner in reaching children and youth, like Tu, with OneHope tools.

Tu, a ten-year-old girl, has been a believer for a few years but was not allowed to attend church regularly, because her mother thought going to church would rob her of time to study. When OneHope's *Kids Evangelism Explosion* program was launched, Tu learned more about God and began participating in other church activities. She went home and shared with her mom what she learned. Through Tu's understanding of, and ability to clearly share, the Gospel message, her mom gained a new understanding of God and became supportive of Tu going to church. Today, Tu is a completely different person who loves sharing the Gospel with others.

Recently, *The GodMan* film was telecast throughout the nation of Nepal. The prayers of those first 868 people have not gone unanswered!

note, names in these testimonies have been disguised for the protection of the individual.

Overlooking the Ngorongoro
crater in Kenya

CHAPTER 11
Return to Africa

In 2013, we revisited Kenya and Tanzania, where I was reminded that Africa holds a special place in my heart. Our initial impression of the natives in the '60's was that they always had warm smiles and gracious hospitality to offer us. This is still true today. In spite of hardships and, in many cases, poverty, Africans in general have a certain *joie de vivre*, (joy of living) which is contagious.

Despite being very busy attending meetings in Kenya and Tanzania, we did get to go on a safari at the Ngorongoro Crater in Kenya. The scene before us looked like it was straight from the movie, *Out of Africa*. We were awed by the wide, sweeping landscape dotted with spreading acacia trees, an occasional towering giraffe or graceful gazelle. It was a peaceful, mystical, surreal experience; we felt like we were peeking into the Garden of Eden, observing God's ordered, beautiful creation.

But, as in the Garden, sin reared its ugly head. A week later, just a few kilometers away, we found ourselves holed up in our hotel as terrorists attacked the upscale Westgate mall in Nairobi, killing more than 60 and injuring more than 200 people.

We were heartbroken, but reminded that where sin abounds, grace abounds much more. The lady cleaning our room feared that we might be nervous and tried to soothe us by saying, "Don't worry. God has everything under control."

And He does!

We heard wonderful stories from our amazing team. In Tanzania alone, more than 6 million children have been reached, and many more in Kenya. God's Word is the only thing that can change the hearts of the next generation.

Afternoon sessions at the Council in Arusha began with enthusiastic singing and dancing. The head Bishop explained, "We are basically an oral culture, as a great percentage of Tanzanians are illiterate. That's why we teach Scripture using music and dancing." This reinforced that we are using effective methods with our programs—depicting God's story through film, pictures and storytelling.

The highlight of the Council was the morning meeting where they invited Bob and me to come forward so leaders could pray over us and our family. In 1960, Bob and I had gone to Africa to tell the story of Jesus. As we were being

Bob and I modeling our traditional African dress

prayed for, I realized that we had come full circle. A powerful presence of God overwhelmed us, and we were blessed and uplifted.

In 1960 in Sierra Leone, we had visited the graves of missionaries who had died from Blackwater fever and malaria. It is said that the Church is built on the blood of the martyrs. We are blessed to be recipients of their sacrifice.

My return to Africa brings good news. The Church in Africa is in good hands; it is alive and well!

Our Family

Our oldest son, David, with kids
Stuart, Katia, Charlotte and Peter

Rob with his beautiful family, Kim,
Natasha and Diandra

Our daughter, Kim, with
her husband Eric

158

Granddaughter Natasha in Ho, Ghana, for the
250 millionth distribution of the Book of Hope

David with Tania,
Stuart and Vass

My handsome grandsons
Ethan and Vass

The boys and I during one of our
evacuations from Lebanon

Epilogue

During one of our three evacuations from Beirut, we were in a small two-bedroom apartment in Europe, and getting on one another's nerves.

Rob did some grievous thing, and his older brother, David, tattled on him. So, Bob was compelled to administer the proper discipline to Rob. During "the laying on of hands," David was in a corner begging, "Stop! You're going to kill my brother." Suddenly, from the other room, I heard them laughing uproariously.

When I went into the "torture room," Rob was holding on to the bed post saying, "HIT ME AGAIN! THAT'S WHAT MAKES ME SO STRONG!"

The situation struck Bob as being so ridiculous, that he and David collapsed in peals of laughter.

I don't think Bob ever used that form of discipline again, but there is a lesson there.

Sometimes God has to hit us over the head a few times to get our attention.

Certainly, there have been many occasions in the lives

of our family when dire circumstances have brought us to our knees. Both Bob and Rob have had detached retinas, which threatened total blindness.

I shall never forget the night after surgery that I spent in the hospital beside Bob. They were to remove his eye bandage the following morning. It was very frightening, as Bob had been blind in one eye from infancy. If the surgery wasn't successful, he would be completely without sight. During the night, we were both awakened to a wonderful presence accompanied by an aroma that permeated the room. We basked in His presence for some time. The next morning when they removed the bandage, he could see!

I've walked through cancer with Bob. Seventeen years ago, he was diagnosed with colon/rectal cancer at stage four. Intensive chemo and radiation followed. Seven years ago, he was diagnosed with prostate cancer, and five years ago, underwent another round of surgery for colon cancer.

Three years ago, while in Central African Republic, Rob contracted a life-threatening strain of E. coli. During the long battle with E. coli, doctors discovered that he also had prostate cancer, requiring surgery. He and his wife Kim showed great strength and grace during this trial. ("That's what makes him so strong.") Thanks to the healing touch of doctors and the prayers of God's people around the world, Bob and Rob are cancer-free as of this writing!

Rob writes about the lessons he and Kim learned during his bout with detached retinas and threatened blindness in his book *Hope Delivered.*

Our oldest son, David, has struggled with kidney failure the last several years. Two years ago, his body rejected a kidney donated by great friend, Shelly Lantz. This kidney had lasted successfully for three years. Presently, David is on dialysis twenty hours a week, awaiting another donor.

I've often heard Bob say, "We all have a destiny. As long as we are fulfilling our calling, the devil can't kill us, and He will not take us."

Worse than the physical "slings and arrows that flesh is 'ere to" are the emotional trials that come our way, sometimes of our own making, and often circumstances that come through living on a fallen planet.

During one of these trying moments when it seemed as if the heavens were brass, I penned these lines:

SILENCE

God, My God, why has Thou forsaken me?
Groaned Jesus on the tree:
As the thorns crushed His brow
And He writhed in agony.

God, are You there? Do You care?
SILENCE
Alone, forsaken, forgotten
To the Son it seemed to be;
But God was working out His plan
For all eternity.

My God, my God, why has Thou forsaken me?
I groaned in my despair;
Are you there? Do you care?
SILENCE
I'm asking not for a mighty wind…a vision
A still small voice would do.
But why this silence?
I know I have Your Word
But I long to hear Your voice…

To feel Your touch…
To experience Your love.

April 1991

Throughout the myriad trips, trials, adventures and adversities that have followed us around the globe, I'm here today penning this book to remind you, and all future generations, that God is faithful. That His promise always holds strong, no matter the circumstances. That God doesn't leave us in silence. He is always present. It is we who need to increase our sensitivity to His voice. He is a real, personal, caring and compassionate God sustaining and blessing His children with unique callings, visions, blessings and skills to advance His kingdom.

In the words of C.S. Lewis:

"God whispers to us in our pleasure;
Speaks in our conscience;
But SHOUTS in our pain.
It is His megaphone to a deaf world."

Diandra, Natasha, Kim
and Rob on the missions field

Afterword

ROB HOSKINS

PRESIDENT, ONEHOPE

It is both sobering and uplifting to read through these pages that chronicle my parents' journey of faith. Some of the stories I remember vividly, others I recall hearing throughout the years but had forgotten 'til now. All of them remind me that a life of ruthless surrender is the life God intends for each of us. Otherwise, we risk missing out on the glory and magnificence He has planned for each of us to experience along the way.

Reading about the genesis of my parents' ministry is a poignant reminder that we build on the foundations of the generations that come before us. Mom and Dad have been faithful, and what they have begun is astounding. The ministry of OneHope was born out of a God-given vision that—year by year—has increased in capacity to achieve the audacious goal that God set for it: "God's Word. Every Child."

Several years ago, my father asked me, "What does mission fulfillment look like?" As I pondered his question, it forced me to do some hard thinking and engage in some serious times of prayer. The challenge seemed daunting—in human terms it felt impossible. But with each passing day, my faith began to grow as I realized that we are living in the "fullness of time." The fulfillment of the Great Commission does not have to be the dream of future generations; it can become the reality of ours.

The growth of a vibrant global Church affords us opportunities my parents never had as they pioneered on their 20th century mission fields. Globalization is shrinking the world into an increasingly interconnected community. New technologies are revolutionizing the speed and scope of how information is being transmitted. We will need the same intractable faith and pioneering spirit of my parents to harness the opportunities of our generation. When we do, the reality of children everywhere having access to Christ's love is nearer than it has ever been before.

As our ministry team began to dream, God gave us a plan—Vision 2030—a goal to tangibly serve the global Church and help actuate their capacity to reach young people in their communities by providing tools to help extend their reach even to the far corners of our planet.

Just as my folks were quick to use innovative tactics and bold to make audacious faith goals, so is the team at OneHope. Whether leveraging print, film, storytelling or developing digital platforms, our mission is as steadfast and clear as ever.

One of the signs of a great leader is whether or not their works transcend their life span. I'm sure that the stories you have just read are proof that my parents' ministry efforts have already made an eternally significant impact! I am convinced that the events and circumstances of their lives were God-ordained to uniquely prepare them to launch a movement that will continue to affect countless destinies as we make God's Word available to every child.

As I read this book, I found myself not only celebrating the lives of my missionary parents, but I also found myself recommitting my life to the truths, values and mission that have guided and directed their lifelong—and still ongoing—ministry.

Bob and I surrounded by friends and family celebrating our 50th wedding anniversary

Acknowledgments

Special thanks to the hundreds of people who have prayed for us and for our children during our fifty-four years of ministry. Many of you woke in the night and felt compelled to intercede on our behalf. As we compared notes afterward, we often found that you had been praying protection over us while we were in the midst of great danger. Due to your obedience, we were delivered.

To the churches and individuals that contribute to our ministry—many in a sacrificial way—we say "gracias," "merci," "spasiba." Without your support, we would not have been able to fulfill the mission God has called us to.

To my brother, David Crabtree and his wife, Dawn, a debt of gratitude. While pastoring in Des Moines in 1980, they took care of our two "refugee boys," David and Rob, while Kim and I were settling in San Jose, California.

To my other brother, Charles Crabtree and his wife, Ramona, who also provided sanctuary for us at Bethel Church, where they pastored. This was a providential place of healing and community. It was great to reconnect with my sister and her husband, Charlotte and Ray Carlson, during this time as well. They are psychologist and teacher, respectively—God knew exactly whom we needed to minister to us!

My dear friend, Juanita Blackburn, who has always encouraged me to write a book. In fact, she edited several articles that have been published in various magazines and are represented in these pages as well.

To Jenna Scott who, along with Linda Whiddon and Patricia Savage, efficient OneHopers, have helped me organize my wandering thoughts the last few months and focus while "I've Just Sat There" in front of my computer. One compiles a lot of "stuff" during 80 years of life!

To so many friends who have impacted and blessed my life; I can't begin to thank you. You know who you are, and I pray God's richest blessings on you and yours.

Notes:

Notes:

Notes:

Notes: